Proclaiming the **Scandal** of the **Cross**

Contemporary Images of the Atonement

Edited by
Mark D. Baker

Baker Academic
Grand Rapids, Michigan

© 2006 by Mark D. Baker

Published by Baker Academic
a division of Baker Publishing Group
P.O. Box 6287, Grand Rapids, MI 49516-6287
www.bakeracademic.com

Printed in the United States of America

Library of Congress Cataloging-in-Publication Data
Proclaiming the scandal of the cross : contemporary images of the atonement / edited by Mark D. Baker.
    p. cm.
    Includes bibliographical references.
    ISBN 10: 0-8010-2742-X (pbk.)
    ISBN 978-0-8010-2742-0 (pbk.)
    1. Atonement. 2. Jesus Christ-Crucifixion. I. Baker, Mark D. (Mark David), 1957-
BT265.3P76 2006
232'.3—dc22   2006024577

Proclaiming the **Scandal** of the Cross

This book is dedicated to my daughters
Julia and Christie

Contents

Contributors

Mark D. Baker is associate professor of mission and theology at Mennonite Brethren Biblical Seminary in Fresno, California. He was a missionary in Honduras for ten years and has authored books in Spanish and English, including *Religious No More: Building Communities of Grace and Freedom*.

Debbie Blue is one of the founding pastors of House of Mercy Church in St. Paul, Minnesota. She is the author of *Sensual Orthodoxy*, a collection of sermons, and is currently at work on a book about how Christians tend to make the Bible an idol and how the Word resists.

Curtis Chang is the teaching pastor at the River Church Community, San Jose, California. He previously served with InterVarsity Christian Fellowship for eight years and is the author of *Engaging Unbelief: A Captivating Strategy from Augustine and Aquinas*.

Doug Frank is a professor at the Oregon Extension, an interdisciplinary program where students can attend to their deepest questions during a semester of intensive reading, writing, and conversation. He attends Lincoln Christian Church in a small community amid the southern Oregon mountains, where he lives and works. He is the author of *Less Than Conquerors: How Evangelicals Entered the Twentieth Century.*

Chris Friesen has been serving in pastoral ministry at Lendrum Mennonite Brethren Church in Edmonton, Alberta, Canada.

Richard B. Hays is the George Washington Ivey Professor of New Testament at Duke Divinity School, Durham, North Carolina. He is an ordained United Methodist minister and author of a number of books including: *The Moral Vision of the New Testament: Community, Cross, New Creation* and *The Conversion of the Imagination: Paul as Interpreter of Israel's Scripture.*

C. S. Lewis was an Anglican layman who taught literature, first at Oxford University and later at Cambridge University. He had been an atheist and converted to Christianity in his midthirties. Lewis wrote poetry, novels, and nonfiction works, and his many books include works on theology, apologetics, and literary criticism. He died in 1963.

Frederica Mathewes-Green is a columnist for Beliefnet.com, and a film reviewer for *National Review Online.* She regularly contributes to *Christianity Today, First Things, Touchstone,* and other publications. Her recent books include: *The Illumined Heart: The Ancient Christian Path of Transformation* and *Facing East: A Pilgrim's Journey into the Mysteries of Orthodoxy.* She is the Khouria (spiritual mother) of Holy Cross Antiochian Orthodox Church near Baltimore, where her husband is the pastor.

Grace Y. May is an ordained minister of the Presbyterian Church (USA). She is currently serving as the associate pastor of the English Ministry at the First Chinese Presbyterian Church in New York City's Chinatown. While living in the Boston area she pastored at the Chinese Christian Church of New England and previously served at the African-American Roxbury Presbyterian Church. She has contributed to *The Global God: Multicultural Evangelical Views of God* and *Growing Healthy Asian-American Churches.*

Brian D. McLaren served for twenty-four years as the founding pastor of Cedar Ridge Community Church, an innovative church near Washington, D.C. More than half of the several hundred people who attend Cedar Ridge were previously unchurched. He has written a number of books including: *The Secret Message of Jesus*; *A Generous Orthodoxy*; and the *A New Kind of Christian* trilogy (www.brianmclaren.net).

Mike McNichols is the pastor of Soulfarers Community, a Vineyard Church in Fullerton, California, that he and a team of friends planted in 1997. He also works with Fuller Theological Seminary's Southern California Extension program. He has worked as an elementary school teacher and principal, and also in marketing. He recently completed a doctoral project—a novel about postmodern evangelism titled, *The Bartender*.

Gwinyai H. Muzorewa, originally from Zimbabwe, is an ordained minister of the United Methodist Church. He is professor of theology and chair of the Religion Department at Lincoln University, Pennsylvania. He has written four books, including *The Origin and Development of African Theology* and *Mwari: The Great Being God*.

Ryan Schellenberg recently graduated from Mennonite Brethren Biblical Seminary in Fresno, California, with an M.A. in New Testament. He is from Hepburn, Saskatchewan, and is pursuing a Ph.D. in New Testament at the Toronto School of Theology.

Luci Shaw was the cofounder and later president of Harold Shaw Publishers and since 1988 has been an adjunct faculty member and Writer in Residence at Regent College, Vancouver, Canada. She lives in Bellingham, Washington, and is a member of St. Paul's Episcopal Church. She is author of numerous books of poetry and prose, including *Water Lines: New and Selected Poems*; *Water My Soul: Cultivating the Interior Life*; and *What the Light Was Like*. She has also coauthored three books with Madeleine L'Engle, including *A Prayer Book for Spiritual Friends*.

Steve Taylor is pastor at Opawa Baptist Church, Christchurch, New Zealand, and lecturer in practical theology at the Bible College of New Zealand. He has planted an emerging church, Graceway Baptist Church, Auckland, New Zealand, and is author of *The Out of Bounds Church? Learning to Create Communities of Faith in a Culture of Change.*

Steve Todd is the founding pastor of Horizons Community Church, a United Methodist Church started in 1996 in suburban Lincoln, Nebraska. He has pastored other Methodist churches in Nebraska since 1981.

Dan Whitmarsh is the lead pastor at Lakebay Community Church (Evangelical Covenant Church) in Lakebay, Washington.

Rowan Williams is the Archbishop of Canterbury. He has written a number of books, including *A Ray of Darkness: Sermons and Reflections* and *Resurrection: Interpreting the Easter Gospel.*

1

Contextualizing the Scandal of the Cross

Mark D. Baker

Since many Christians today can easily offer an explanation of the meaning of Jesus's death on the cross, they find it hard to understand the bewilderment and confusion of the two disciples described at the end of Luke's Gospel on their way to Emmaus. They had understood Jesus's ministry in terms borrowed from expectation of a liberator like Moses;[1] hence, they had no interpretive tools for making sense of his execution at the hands of the Romans. Paul, however, would likely find it quite understandable that the disciples were confused and find it harder to understand that the cross does not scandalize us. In 1 Corinthians 1:18–25, the apostle outlines a perspective on the cross that many of us have learned to overlook. Here he testifies to the lunacy of the cross for first-century Romans, matched by its ignominious character among the Jewish people.[2]

The Christian proclamation of a crucified malefactor was moronic to persons weaned on a love of learning, virtuousness, and aesthetic pleasure. The Messiah, like Moses before him, should evidence the power of God in ways that legitimate his status and augur deliverance from the tyranny and oppressiveness of imperial subjugation. In that context the cross has the appearance of absurdity, not of "good news." The message of the cross calls for a worldview shift of colossal proportions because it subverts conventional, taken-for-granted ways of thinking and knowing.

Joel Green and I wrote *Recovering the Scandal of the Cross: Atonement in New Testament and Contemporary Contexts* with the conviction that the most common contemporary explanation of the atonement, penal satisfaction, has in some contexts muted the scandal of the cross, in other settings inappropriately scandalized people, and in still other circumstances made the saving significance of the cross and resurrection incomprehensible.[3] Unfortunately, many see penal satisfaction as the sole way of proclaiming the saving significance of the cross. We argued that an important first step in recovering the scandal of the cross is to recognize the diversity of atonement images used both in the New Testament and in the teaching and preaching of the church since the first century. We sought not just to display that diversity, however, but also to ask what we can learn from the New Testament and church history that can guide us in our articulation of the atonement in diverse contexts today.

We are thankful that many have found the book liberating and illuminating and have told us how it has helped them to experience the challenge and good news of the scandalous cross of Jesus Christ. We are also grateful for the conversation the book has generated. Although much of that has centered on biblical and theological issues, the question of articulation has also been prominent. In fact, many have repeatedly intimated to us that they had given up on preaching the atonement but have found in our work renewed challenge and resources for reflecting anew on the saving significance of the cross. Others have said something like this: "You have led me to think quite differently about the atonement, but now how do I preach about the atonement?" Or, "Great material, but can you give me a five-minute explanation that I can use in evangelism?" This new volume, *Proclaiming the Scandal of the Cross*, is my response to those questions. It presents examples of people in concrete settings using images and stories to communicate the saving significance of the cross and resurrection.

In this introductory chapter I first aim to summarize some key points from *Recovering the Scandal of the Cross*, including guidelines for contextualization. Then I discuss why this book offers alternatives to the penal satisfaction theory of the atonement through responding to some critiques of *Recovering the Scandal*, and through explaining how I imagine this book being helpful to people with different atonement theologies. Finally, I give a brief explanation of the format of the book and how the presentations in the book relate to each other and the project we sketched in *Recovering the Scandal*.

NEW TESTAMENT ATONEMENT TEACHING: AN OVERVIEW

Constructive and missional aims drove our survey of New Testament atonement teaching in *Recovering the Scandal of the Cross*. We did not seek simply to report what Luke, Paul, or John stated about the atonement, but also to observe their theological and missiological concerns in order to communicate better the saving significance of the cross and resurrection in our own time and contexts.

The New Testament contains a rich diversity of atonement teaching and imagery. Indeed, the contextual rootedness of the New Testament is perhaps nowhere on display more than in its atonement theology. Drawing on the language and thought patterns of Israel's religion and life experiences within the larger Greco-Roman world, these writers struggled to make sense of Jesus's crucifixion. Within the pages of the New Testament, the saving significance of the death of Jesus is represented chiefly (though not exclusively) via five constellations of images. Each set of imagery is borrowed from significant spheres of public life in ancient Palestine and the larger Greco-Roman world: the court of law (for justification), commercial dealings (redemption), personal relationships (reconciliation, whether among individuals or groups), worship (sacrifice), and the battleground (triumph over evil).

Why does the New Testament enlist so many images for its atonement theology? First, because language for the atonement is metaphorical, and given the nature of metaphor, it is difficult to imagine that one soteriological model could express all that one may truly say about the saving significance of Jesus's death. Hence, even if Christians have always spoken with one voice in their general affirmation of Jesus as our Savior, already in the New Testament, and certainly since, readers have understood this affirmation in various ways.

A second reason for the plurality of New Testament images for the atonement is pastoral. In what language one construes the efficacy of Jesus's death is dependent in part on the needs one hopes to address. Chris Tuckett has similarly observed, "Very different models and categories are used to describe the 'lost' condition of the human race prior to Christ. . . . Different descriptions of the human situation inevitably lead to different explanations of how this has been altered by the work of Christ."[4] If people are lost, they need to be found. If they are oppressed by hostile powers, they need to be delivered. If they exist in a state of enmity, they need to be reconciled. And so on.

Third, the early Christians used a plurality of metaphors to draw out the salvific significance of Jesus's death and resurrection because of wider cultural considerations. If hearers in ever-expanding cultural circles are to grasp the message of salvation, then leaders must articulate that message in culture-specific ways.

Thus, a central and fundamental guideline we learn from the New Testament authors is the importance of using a variety of images to proclaim the scandal of the cross: different contexts require different images.

Just as highlighting the distinctness of individual writings and metaphors provides us valuable guidance, so too looking at common themes of the whole provides theological guidelines as we work to articulate the meaning of Jesus's death and resurrection in new contexts. In *Recovering the Scandal of the Cross*, then, we attempted to derive orientation points from the New Testament as landmarks for constructive work in atonement theology. Although they leave plenty of room for creative theological reflection, these four guidelines also provide crucial points of orientation in our reflection.

The first of these turns the spotlight on the human predicament. One may articulate "lostness" in a variety of ways—blindness, deafness, hard-heartedness, slavery to an evil power, enmity, and so on—but one of the constants in the equation of biblical thinking about the atonement is the acute need of the human community. Humanity lacks the wherewithal to save itself and needs help (salvation, redemption, deliverance, and so on) from the outside, from God.

A second coordinate is the necessity of human response that flows out of the gracious act of God. The salvific work of God has not yet run its full course, but the lives of God's people must already begin to reflect the new reality (new creation) to which God is moving history. We are saved *from* bad things, it is true, but we are also saved *for* something. Atonement theology in the New Testament does not simply hold tightly to the work of Christ; it also opens wide its arms to embrace and guide the lives of Christians. Believers—having been redeemed, reconciled, delivered, bought, justified, and so on—are now released and empowered to reflect in their lives the quality of life exemplified by their Savior. This life is modeled after the cross and has service as its basic orientation. We must not separate atonement *theology* from *ethics*.

Between the human predicament and the imperative of human response is the divine drama, the ultimate manifestation of God's love. This is the third coordinate: God, acting on the basis of his covenant love, on his own initiative, was at work in the cross of Christ for human salvation. The New Testament portrays Golgotha along two story lines—one with God as (acting) subject, the other with Jesus as (acting) subject. It will not do, therefore, to characterize the atonement as God's punishment falling on Christ (God as subject, Christ as object) or as Christ's appeasement or persuasion of God (Christ as subject, God as object). At the same time, however paradoxical it may seem, what happened on the cross for our atonement was, according to the New Testament, a consequence of God's initiative, a demonstration of divine love. As Paul summarizes, employing one model among many possibilities, "God was in Christ, reconciling the world unto himself" (2 Cor. 5:19 KJV). Again, "God proves [displays] his love for us in that while we still were sinners Christ died for us" (Rom. 5:8 NRSV).

Fourth, and as a corollary to the three previous themes, New Testament atonement theology accords privilege to no one group over another. What happened on the cross was of universal significance—in the language of the day, for Jew and Gentile, for slave and free, for male and female (Gal. 3:28). The cross was the expression of God's grace for all, for all persons as well as for all creation. Atonement theology thus repudiates ancient and modern attempts to segregate people away from the gracious invitation of God, to possess as one's own the gift of God available to all humanity, and even to presume that the work of God in Christ is focused only on humanity, without regard for the whole cosmos.

We can also gain missiological guidelines from the New Testament authors for the task of articulating the atonement. First, we must avoid the temptation to simply read their words and metaphors into our world. Rather, we must seek to use words and metaphors that communicate similar content in our setting; we must follow their example of drawing on images from the everyday experience of people's lives. For instance, in many parts of the world today, if one wants to use the metaphor of sacrifice to communicate the atonement, one would first have to explain how a first-century Jew might understand sacrifice. Yet even having the information about sacrifices does not mean the metaphor would fully communicate to or connect with people for whom sacrifices are totally foreign. In contrast, however, a tribal society that still uses sacrifices today might readily understand the sacrificial metaphor as the biblical materials develop it.

If we would be faithful to Scripture, we too must continuously seek out metaphors, new and old, that speak effectively and specifically to our various worlds. Yet, if we would follow in the path of the New Testament writers, the metaphors we deploy would be at home in our settings, but never too comfortable here. Those writers sought, and urge us to seek, not only to be understood by people and social systems around us, but also to shape them. Moreover, we would not eschew earlier models or the reality to which they point, but would carry on our constructive work fully in conversation with and under the guidance of the Scriptures of Israel and the church, and of apostolic testimony.

A Historical and Theological Overview of Atonement Teaching

Although in many Christian circles a penal satisfaction theory of the atonement is understood to be *the* explanation of how the cross provides salvation, even a brief historical look at atonement thinking points to a different reality. First, there have been a number of different explanations of the atonement. Second, the satisfaction view of the atonement was not a common explanation of the atonement during the first thousand years of church history.[5] Just as our reading of the New Testament invited us to consider using various images to communicate the scandal of the cross, so a broad look at church history leads us in a similar direction, or at least gives us permission to explore alternative explanations.

Let me briefly sketch three main streams of atonement thinking: conflict-victory (or *Christus Victor*), penal satisfaction, and moral influence. Each of the three has numerous variations, and some approaches to the atonement do not fit neatly into one of these three categories. But for the purposes of this summary, I will paint with a broad brush.[6]

CONFLICT-VICTORY

The conflict-victory motif of the atonement describes the cross and resurrection as a conflict between God and the powers of evil, death, or the devil. This was the most common view of the atonement during the first millennium of the church. It remains the predominant atonement teaching in the Eastern church. Gustaf Aulén's work in the mid-twentieth century contributed to a resurgence of interest in this current of thinking.[7] Although some versions of the *Christus Victor* model have been critiqued for portraying God as using trickery to snare Satan, with Jesus as the bait, many other versions of *Christus Victor*, both contemporary and from the patristic era, avoid this sort of detailed speculation and develop theologically sound images of liberation, rescue, or defeat/victory.[8]

The image of the cross as a victory over the powers of evil and the metaphor of ransom or redemption are explicitly developed in the New Testament.[9] This stream of atonement thinking does well at following the guidelines listed above, which we developed from the New Testament. The conflict-victory motif is able to communicate clearly the acute need of humanity for liberation from enslavement to sin and the powers of evil, at both a corporate and personal level, and it does so without presenting Christ's victory in a way that privileges certain persons or groups over others. Jesus's life of obedience, and not just at the moment of crucifixion, is integral to many forms of this motif; those presentations lend themselves to reflection on the ethical implications of Jesus's saving activity since the way he lived his life is an integral part of his saving work. There is no hint of Christ appeasing God the Father, nor of the Father punishing the Son. Indeed, Origen (ca. 185–254), an early proponent of this view, strongly dismisses the notion that Jesus Christ was supplying a ransom payment to God the Father.

Penal Satisfaction

As commonly understood, the satisfaction theory of the atonement states that sin prevents humans from being in relationship to God because God is holy. Since God is just, he cannot simply forgive human sin without first requiring punishment or payment of an appropriate penalty. God, however, provides a solution. God the Father sends his Son to earth to suffer the punishment we deserve by dying on the cross. This satisfies God's justice, and since Jesus has paid the penalty for us, God can regard us as not guilty. If we believe that we are sinners deserving of divine judgment, but that Jesus died in our place, then we can be in relationship with God and go to heaven.

In his book *Cur Deus homo* (*Why God Became Man*) Anselm of Canterbury (1033–1109) developed the concept of the cross as satisfaction. He sought to answer the question of the book's title not by using biblical terminology, but by borrowing concepts and images from the medieval world of lords and vassals. In that setting, a vassal who did not fulfill the requirements of an oath must offer something to satisfy the offended lord. The society saw it as improper if a lord did not demand redress from a guilty vassal or take revenge against another lord who had in some way offended him. Anselm, therefore, merits our praise for doing what I have proposed above, not just mimicking biblical language and images, but also seeking to use images easily understood in his context. We might say, though, that in some ways Anselm overcontextualized. He allowed his experience of medieval life, its logic, and its conventional wisdom to have an overwhelming influence for shaping his model of the atonement.

The greatest problem in relation to the satisfaction model, however, is not Anselm, but those who came after him and stripped his presentation of its medieval garb.[10] These inter-preters of Anselm, perhaps unwittingly, took from him certain core ideas and from their own day added legal terms and ideas alien to his, then presented the result, *penal* satisfaction, as *the* biblical explanation of the atonement.

A great strength of the penal satisfaction theory of the atone-ment is that one can easily explain it to someone from a guilt-based—rather than shame-based—society, to those whose under-standing of justice is shaped by approaches to criminal justice in the contemporary West. If one reads the Bible through the lens of such a society, then Scripture appears to support the penal satisfaction theory. The fact, however, that this explanation of the atonement fails to fully follow the guidelines listed above can lead one to wonder if the lens is leading to a misreading of the biblical text. In its classical and popular forms, penal satisfaction has one member of the Trinity punishing another member of the Trinity. In a penal satisfaction model, something outside of God circumscribes God's ability to love and relate to humans: an abstract concept of justice instructs God as to how God must behave. This view can easily lead people to pic-ture a God who has a vindictive character, who finds it much easier to punish than to forgive. As responses from readers of *Recovering the Scandal of the Cross* have demonstrated to me, although a penal satisfaction explanation of the atonement need not necessarily lead to such a troublesome view of God, it has repeatedly done so.

The penal satisfaction theory of the atonement takes sin quite seriously in that it presents sin as a barrier between God and humans. Yet its concept of sin is anemic in that it portrays sin above all in individualistic terms of moral failure or transgression of a law. Although it serves to provide freedom from guilt, this view fails to connect sufficiently with the day-to-day realities of faithful discipleship since it addresses our reconciliation with God at an abstract level: what changes through the cross is a legal ruling. According to the logic of the model, one could be saved through penal substitution without experiencing a fundamental reorientation of one's life.

Indeed, ethically, this model has little to offer. It draws no significance from Jesus's conflict with the powers of his day and their putting him to death. It sees no meaning in the Gospels' affirmation that Jesus's lifestyle led to his death. Instead, it merely holds as significant that he lived without sinning and that he died. This model concretely presents only one aspect of Jesus's life: his physical suffering, which helps to validate that the penalty was sufficient. Unfortunately, then, in calling people to imitate Christ, this model has been co-opted too easily in order to glorify suffering and encourage passive tolerance of abuse.

In the end, a penal satisfaction presentation of the atonement can too easily lead to a situation in which we might conclude that Jesus came to save us from God. Proponents of penal substitution would certainly protest and explicitly state that because God loved us, he sent his Son to die for us. And, as I will discuss later, able theologians have well-articulated views of penal satisfaction that seek to maintain the unity of the Trinity and strongly affirm God's love. Unfortunately, however, most Christians do not read the carefully nuanced versions of penal satisfaction found in theology texts! Instead, they hear (or sing) explanations of the cross that make it easier to conceive of a God who punishes with vindictive retribution—a God from whom we need to be saved.

MORAL INFLUENCE

Peter Abelard (1079–1142), a contemporary of Anselm, argued that Jesus's death was neither a payment to nor victory over the devil, nor a satisfaction of a debt owed to God. Abelard understood Jesus's life and death as a demonstration of God's love that moves sinners to repent and love God and thus become more righteous:

> Now it seems to us that we have been justified by the blood of Christ and reconciled to God in this way: through this unique act of grace manifested to us—in that his Son has taken upon himself our nature and persevered therein in teaching us by word and

example even unto death—he has more fully bound us to himself by love; with the result that our hearts should be enkindled by such a gift of divine grace, and true charity should not now shrink from enduring anything for him.[11]

Many of those who advocate this position do not articulate it in the same way as Abelard, but like him they view the saving action of the cross as primarily subjective: a change that occurs within humans.

The moral influence theory of the atonement helpfully highlights the subjective aspect of Christ's atoning work, which is present in the Bible but had received minimal attention in previous atonement writing.[12] It would be better, however, if one presented the subjective influence of the cross as a missing element from atonement thinking, rather than as *the* answer to the question of why God became a human. The moral influence theory leaves a number of issues hanging in the air. For instance, although Abelard does include Jesus's death as part of what moves us to love, the theory could function logically without the cross. Moral influence correctly contests the concept of a vindictive, punishing God, but often does so by speaking loudly of God's love and rather softly of God's judgment, instead of depicting God's judgment as part of God's love and distinguishing it from vindictive retribution.

Grace plays a significant role in this theory: God takes the initiative to act in a way that will lead to our reconciliation. Yet some proponents of this position display overconfidence in the human capacity to bring about our salvation. For instance, Abelard assumes that, awakened by the example of God's love, we can reach a point of living righteously. Sin appears as a relative and surmountable barrier for Abelard, in contrast to the view of sin as an insurmountable barrier in other explanations.[13]

The ethical character of the moral influence theory is more pronounced than the other models; it requires not only that Jesus lived an exemplary sinless life but also that humans live differently in response to the example of Jesus's life. In addition to the abstract nature of his description of these changes, a significant weakness of Abelard's model is its individualistic character. The focus is on Jesus's life and death moving individuals to love and to be reconciled with God. These individuals indeed could then come together and form Christian community in a voluntary way, but neither the community-forming nature of Christ's work nor the sense of reconciliation with others that is part of one's reconciliation with God appear to be integral to Abelard's explanation of the atonement.

GENERAL COMMENTS

These three approaches provide different explanations of how the cross provides salvation. The conflict-victory motif of the atonement describes the cross and resurrection as directed toward death, sin as a power, powers of evil, and/or the devil, to liberate people. The penal satisfaction theory of the atonement describes the cross as directed toward God, to pay a debt. The moral influence theory of the atonement describes the life and death of Jesus as directed toward the human individual, to provoke change for reconciliation.

If any one of these three is advocated as *the* one correct explanation of the atonement, then aspects of God's saving action through the life, death, and resurrection of Jesus are at best downplayed and at worst ignored. In *Recovering the Scandal of the Cross*, therefore, we did not develop a new theory of the atonement that seeks to address weaknesses we see in other theories; rather, we advocated using a variety of metaphors and images of atonement, just as the New Testament writers did. Thus, although I have just offered a pointed critique of the moral influence theory of the atonement, in this book I have included some chapters that use what one might call a subjective presentation of the atonement. Like moral influence, such testimonies center on the cross's saving influence on humans rather than on an objective presentation that focuses on a change outside of humans. What I have not included, and would continue to argue against, is a presentation that portrays the cross's affect on humans as capturing the totality of its saving significance.

Although use of terms such as "subjective" and "objective" can be helpful in making distinctions between different presentations of the atonement, I will do so infrequently. It too easily implies that an image of the atonement communicates only the objective work or only a subjective work of the cross and resurrection; on the contrary, these two are often not so neatly separated.

SUBSTITUTIONARY ATONEMENT

A number of people have criticized *Recovering the Scandal of the Cross* for its alleged rejection of the idea of substitutionary atonement. This critique has surprised me. Although we raise a number of critical concerns about the model of penal substitutionary atonement, we do not reject the idea of substitutionary atonement. As Green and I wrote, "Many, including both proponents and opponents of penal substitution, have a narrow definition of substitution that does not allow for any understanding other than a legal/penal one that pictures Jesus standing in the place of humans and suffering God's retributive punishment that was to have been directed at humans."[14] As it has become increasingly obvious to me, many assume that "substitutionary atonement" is merely a shorthand way to refer to "penal substitutionary atonement." Unfortunately, to accept the two as synonymous hinders one from seeing and using nonpenal, but substitutionary, imagery.

Substitution is a broad term that one can use with reference to a variety of metaphors. For instance, as C. Norman Kraus explains:

> A ransom or hostage is a kind of substitute. A go-between is a kind of substitute. A leader who identifies with his/her people and represents their cause is a substitute as well as one player who takes the place of another. Further if we think in terms of substitute payment there are different types. The payment may be a restitution of what was taken, a payment of bad debt, the payment of ransom, or it might be payment of a legally-prescribed penalty (a fine) in place of the offender.[15]

One clear example of a nonpenal substitutionary model is Irenaeus's recapitulation theory. With Romans 5 echoing in the background, it views Jesus as fulfilling a representative role for all humanity and, in contrast to Adam, resisting and triumphing over the devil at every step—finally conquering death itself. In this book you will find additional examples of atonement presentations that are alternatives to the penal satisfaction imagery, but are still substitutionary in nature.

I understand why, in the past, evangelical theologians reacted against theories of the atonement, like the moral influence theory, that attempted to communicate a complete explanation of the atonement, but lacked a substitutionary sense of Jesus doing something for us that we could not do for ourselves.[16] I share this concern. I find it unfortunate, however, that in reacting to the shortcomings of other models of atonement thinking, many have presented penal satisfaction theory as *the* only alternative. Doing so not only downplays or ignores subjective aspects of biblical atonement imagery; it also defines penal satisfaction as the sole way of interpreting the substitutionary character of Jesus's death. In an effort to help create semantic space for readers to differentiate between the general category, substitutionary atonement, and the specific type, penal substitution, I frequently used the phrase "penal satisfaction" to refer to the latter.

A WORD TO DIFFERENT TYPES OF READERS

I recognize that readers of this book have differing perspectives on the atonement, so I want to identify five points on the spectrum of atonement thinking and offer a word on how I imagine people at each point might find this book helpful.

Atonement-less Teaching and Preaching

Some people have reacted so strongly to penal satisfaction atonement imagery that they have opted to leave the atonement out of their teaching and preaching. For some, this is explicit and intentional. For others, it is by default. It is not that they state they have opted for an atonement-less Christianity, but they simply lack alternative language or imagery. If they do preach or teach about the cross, they might focus, for instance, on the cross as a model of nonviolence to imitate, but they do not address its saving significance.

Although I may share some of their criticisms of penal satisfaction, I nevertheless view this response as problematic. In fact, concern over atonement-less Christianity was one of the principal reasons we wrote *Recovering the Scandal of the Cross*. We hoped that, through the book, people holding this position would see that penal satisfaction is but one option for explaining the atonement, and that the Bible, church history, and contemporary theologians offer alternatives. I hope that this volume's concrete examples of nonpenal satisfaction images of the atonement will help people who currently do not preach and teach about the atonement to imagine ways they can do so and will motivate them to do so.

Looking for Alternatives to Penal Satisfaction

At another point on the spectrum we find readers who have decided that not only is penal satisfaction theory not the one correct explanation of the atonement, but also in fact it has significant problems and does not cohere well with biblical teaching on salvation. Although those in this position have clarity on their critique, they do not have clarity on alternatives. They ask, "What do I preach now? What story can I tell to explain the atonement to youth? How do I portray the saving significance of the cross in an evangelistic conversation?" This book will provide examples of alternatives and thus help people move beyond knowing what they do not want to do, but not knowing what to replace it with.

Looking for Help in Contextualizing the Atonement

People at this point on the spectrum may be uncertain in their evaluation of penal satisfaction, but they are convinced of the importance of seeking to develop atonement presentations that connect with as well as challenge people in a given context. They recognize that traditional presentations of penal satisfaction will not adequately connect with hearers or challenge in all contexts today. Hence, they are eager to work at alternative presentations.

With reference to *Recovering the Scandal of the Cross*, the chapter that most engaged people in this category seemed to be our summary of Norman Kraus's work as a missionary in Japan. Many have commented on Kraus's efforts at articulating the saving significance of the cross and resurrection in terms of shame rather than guilt; he had found that atonement presentations centering on liberation from guilt did not connect with the Japanese. This book contains presentations from a variety of contexts, including a number that address the issue of shame. I therefore hope that readers seeking alternatives will be both encouraged and enabled in their efforts to contextualize the atonement.

Looking for Alternatives in Addition to Penal Satisfaction

People at this point on the spectrum agree that penal satisfaction is not the one correct atonement model. Unlike the second group above, however, this group does not reject penal satisfaction.[17] Hans Boersma is an excellent example of this position. On *Recovering the Scandal of the Cross*, he states: "Green and Baker are helpful when they draw attention to the notions of shame and honor that need to complement those of guilt and justice; and we do well to learn from their understanding of the different voices in the one New Testament choir that make up a delicate harmony of 'wonderful hints of powerful melodies contending with countermelodies.'"[18]

He then acknowledges that listening only to the singing of penal substitution has had negative affects, and therefore he welcomes adding other voices to the choir. In contrast to the second position, however, he wants penal satisfaction to continue to sing in the choir. For those in this position, I trust that this book provides help in adding to the choir.

Penal Satisfaction Only

To continue the metaphor, I know that some people see no need for a choir. For them, the penal satisfaction soloist is enough. Although I have aimed this book at those looking for a choir, not just a soloist, all are welcome to listen to the various "singers" in the book. My hope is that, for some in this position, reading the actual atonement presentations might help them see the value of having a choir—using a variety of metaphors of the atonement.

RESPONDING TO A FEW QUESTIONS

Although this book offers alternatives to the penal satisfaction model of the atonement, it does not pretend to present a thorough argument for why we need alternatives nor how I can claim that penal satisfaction is not biblical. For that, I point readers to *Recovering the Scandal of the Cross*. Although a critique of penal satisfaction is by no means the main focus of that book, it is understandable that proponents of penal satisfaction have raised the most questions about that strand of the book. Addressing these questions is not the purpose of *Proclaiming the Scandal of the Cross*. In fact, as stated in the previous paragraph, people with a penal-satisfaction-only view of the atonement are not the intended audience of this book. I would, however, like to engage two questions people have raised.

Why Not Interact with the Best Examples of Penal Satisfaction?

Although in *Recovering the Scandal of the Cross* we did refer to some contemporary proponents of penal satisfaction, we chose Charles Hodge's atonement theology as the exemplar of that position. Some have asked why we did not interact with more nuanced articulations of penal satisfaction written by some contemporary theologians. That is a fair question. We chose a "classical" rather than contemporary articulation of the position to parallel what we did for *Christus Victor* and moral influence theory. More significantly, however, when we wrote *Recovering the Scandal of the Cross*, our first concern was not so much the scholarly discussion of atonement theology, the sort that occupies professional theologians. We were more concerned about the way leaders conceive and articulate the atonement at the popular level, leaders such as Sunday school teachers, Christian camp counselors, preachers, evangelists. In our judgment, choosing Hodge allowed us to interact with a classical articulation of penal satisfaction that has been and continues to be quite influential (his work remains in print today), as well as interact with a version of penal satisfaction that mirrors well what is articulated at the popular level today.

I agree with our critics that some contemporary scholarly versions of penal satisfaction avoid some of the problems we highlight. Two recent examples are Hans Boersma and Kevin Vanhoozer.[19] Boersma argues for the use of not only penal substitution, but also the full range of atonement explanations found in Christian tradition. He seeks to articulate penal substitution in a way that lessens its tendency toward the "juridicizing, individualizing, and de-historicizing of the cross."[20] Vanhoozer seeks to explain a penal substitutionary understanding of the atonement not in terms of an economy of exchange, but an economy of excess—an excess of justice and love. I appreciate and respect both of these formulations of penal substitution. Although I have some points of disagreement with them, I consider them positive contributions to the church's atonement thinking. It was not works like theirs that motivated me to write *Recovering the Scandal of the Cross*; rather, it was what I heard and read at the popular level.

Unfortunately, unnuanced versions of penal satisfaction, with the full range of problems to which we have drawn attention, are certainly present and thriving at the popular level—in sermons, tracts, around campfires, in popular praise songs, and in small-group Bible studies.[21] I therefore remain convinced that the most common presentations of penal satisfaction must be critiqued, and alternatives must be developed. Seeking change at the popular level is my concern and focus in this book.

But the Bible Says . . .

A group of questions addressed to me, in reviews as well as in conversation with pastors, students, and laypeople, start with the introductory phrase, "But the Bible says. . . ." Readers point to verses that "clearly" communicate a penal satisfaction view of the atonement and ask, "How can you say that penal satisfaction is not biblical?" I might make a variety of responses. For example, I can point to the hermeneutical questions attendant to interacting with biblical texts. If, as I think, we must take individual texts seriously not only on their own terms but also within their wider contexts, including their relation to the canon of Christian Scripture, then at the end of the day this discussion cannot rest merely on lexical arguments or on the results of grammatical-historical exegesis. At the same time, I acknowledge that we could have given more attention to exegetical issues related to a few specific texts typically used to support a penal satisfaction theory. Thereby we could demonstrate the possibility of alternative, plausible ways to read those texts—ways demonstrating that such texts do not so readily lead to penal satisfaction as people often assume.

A first step in imagining this possibility might be recognizing that, for centuries, Christians preached and taught the message of Christianity without the gospel leading them to the inescapable conclusion of penal satisfaction. It is noteworthy that Orthodox Christians still read their Bibles without finding this theory. Frederica Mathewes-Green, writing from an Orthodox perspective, states that with few exceptions Christian writers before Anselm believed that God did in fact freely forgive us like the father in the Prodigal Son parable. She asks:

> Would Christians really have misunderstood their salvation for a thousand years? Did the people Paul wrote his letters to have no idea what he was talking about? Did the early martyrs die without understanding the Cross that saved them? . . . Before Anselm, the problem salvation addresses is seen as located in us. We are infected by death as a result of Adam's fall. This infection will cause us to be spiritually sick and to commit sin. . . . Christ offers a rescue. . . . With Anselm, the problem of salvation is between us and God (we have a debt we can't pay). After Anselm, it is even sometimes formulated as *within* God (His wrath won't be quenched until the debt is paid).[22]

She observes, "When we speak of Christ paying with his blood, we don't necessarily have to imagine a two-sided transaction." She gives a contemporary example. If a policeman rescued some hostages but was wounded in the process, we might say, "He paid with his blood." "But that doesn't mean the kidnappers were left gloating over a vial of blood."[23]

A glance at Christian history and a reading of Scripture through Orthodox lenses invites us to imagine other possibilities as we look at texts that appear "clearly" to communicate penal satisfaction. Looking at the broader biblical text and observing texts in tension with penal satisfaction may be a helpful next step in imagining other readings of "penal satisfaction texts." Raymund Schwager draws attention to a few of these points of tension:

> According to the doctrine of infinite satisfaction, one is indeed fully justified in speaking of a transfer of Christ's merits to all repentant sinners. But this overlooks that it is not just the punishment for sins but the sins themselves that were transferred to the Holy One. Yet it is precisely this process that the New Testament

writings stress so clearly. Furthermore, the image of God that stood behind the long-accepted satisfaction theory can hardly be brought into harmony with the father to whom Jesus repeatedly referred. The parables of the prodigal son (Luke 15:11–32) and the merciless creditor (Matt. 18:23–35) make it clear that God forgives without demanding satisfaction and payment in return. He demands only that we forgive others as unconditionally as we are granted unconditional mercy. . . . The Gospel of Matthew goes so far as to put the parable of the merciless creditor in direct connection with Jesus' command to his disciples to forgive without limit. . . . If Jesus demands of human beings a limitless forgiveness, then the Father whom he makes known must be even more willing to do so.[24]

Although Paul has written a number of the texts that many would point to as "clearly" describing salvation through penal satisfaction, we can also find texts in tension with penal satisfaction in Paul. Some clearly portray *Christus Victor* imagery (e.g., 1 Cor. 2:6–8; Col. 2:15); others communicate ideas in direct tension with the logic of penal satisfaction. For instance, observe the direction of the reconciling work in this verse: "All this is from God, who reconciled us to himself through Christ" (2 Cor. 5:18 NIV). In contrast, penal satisfaction describes the cross's action as directed toward God and changing something that allows God to be reconciled to us. William Placher observes:

Focusing on God's need to be reconciled to us gets things backwards, from the New Testament standpoint. For Paul, it is we who need to be reconciled to God, not the other way around. God's love endures; it is our sin that has broken our relationship with God; it is we who like sheep have gone astray. The barriers that have to be broken down in reconciliation were built from our side.[25]

The tension between these biblical passages and penal satisfaction can buttress the possibility that there may be other ways of reading the texts that people suppose are clearly teaching penal satisfaction.

On the other hand, even if one wants to imagine other readings of these texts, it is often quite difficult to do so if one has always read them, or heard them read, as texts describing penal satisfaction. For example, a student in a Christology class who was both engaged by and sympathetic to the perspective outlined in *Recovering the Scandal of the Cross* stated, "I want to agree with what you are saying, but I was reading Romans, and there it is plain and simple, 'The wages of sin is death' (6:23). It's penal satisfaction. How can you say the cross is not a penalty for our sins that God demands?" The student could imagine no other possibility.

There are, however, other ways of reading this verse. First, we have options concerning whom we picture as the paymaster, the one making the payment of death. Penal satisfaction pictures God delivering this payment. One could just as easily picture Satan as doling out death. Or we could also imagine sin itself paying the wage of death. The latter two provide images of atonement quite different from penal satisfaction. Second, we can picture the payment taking place in different ways. Penal satisfaction would tend to view it as a punishment given out by a judge (God) in response to a damnable life. Alternatively, we could read this verse as saying that a sinful life causes death. It is what sin pays, that to which sin leads. Sin gives death; God's gift is life. In this latter picture death is an integrated consequence of the sinful life itself. Our sin leads to death. Jesus enters into our world and lives in a way that causes him to suffer the ultimate consequence of sin (death, rejection), not because God demanded that penalty in order to be appeased, but because that is what our alienation causes, that to which it leads. But the gift of God, the response of God, is life and forgiveness.

What of a text such as Romans 3:24–25? These verses invite lengthy consideration, but I briefly outline a few considerations. First, the text:

> [All are] justified freely by his grace through the redemption that is in Christ Jesus: Whom God hath set forth to be a propitiation through faith in his blood, to declare his righteousness. . . . (KJV)

> They are justified by his grace as a gift, through the redemption which is in Christ Jesus, whom God put forward as an expiation by his blood, to be received by faith. This was to show God's righteousness. . . . (RSV)

> [All] are justified freely by his grace through the redemption that came by Christ Jesus. God presented him as a sacrifice of atone-

ment, through faith in his blood. He did this to demonstrate his justice. . . . (NIV)

They are now justified by his grace as a gift, through the redemption that is in Christ Jesus, whom God put forward as a sacrifice of atonement by his blood, effective through faith. He did this to show his righteousness. . . . (NRSV)

In these lines many hear a statement of the basic tenets of penal satisfaction. If we read the phrase "sacrifice of atonement" through the lens of penal satisfaction (or with the KJV's term "propitiation" echoing in our mind), then we can easily reach the conclusion that this text clearly teaches that the cross brings salvation through penal satisfaction. Are there other ways to understand "sacrifice of atonement"? The translators of the RSV thought so, and this led them to chose the word "expiation" rather than "propitiation" or "sacrifice of atonement."

The Greek word *hilastērion* can be translated variously: "mercy seat" (or "place of atonement in the holy of holies"), "propitiation" (atonement through an offering of appeasement that turns away divine wrath), or "expiation" (atonement through the covering over or obliterating of sin). Heated debate swirls around the translation of this word.[26] The New International Version and New Revised Standard Version have done well to use "sacrifice of atonement" and thus allow for either interpretation (propitiation or expiation). I bring up the debate, and the various translations, to highlight the reality that to read this verse as describing Jesus paying the penalty of our sins and appeasing God's wrath is a possible reading, but not the only possible reading. One can also easily interpret this text in a way congruent with 2 Corinthians 5:18: the cross is an action aimed not at satisfying God's need to punish, but at overcoming a barrier on the human side that prevents relationship with God.

I have commented on only one word in these verses, and a reader might quickly point out that this atoning act demonstrates God's justice or righteousness, and thereby one might claim that is the key to showing us how to translate and interpret *hilastērion*. Here again, however, we can read the text in different ways. From the perspective of penal satisfaction, God demonstrates justice or righteousness by carrying out the punishment humans deserve, which then allows God to pardon our sins while still satisfying a standard of justice that demands punishment. But one can argue that this view places the transformative significance of Christ's death in the wrong place. What is required is not a transformation within God's heart toward sinners; rather, justice comes through a transformation of sinful human existence before God. And to present those two options is not even to bring up the issue of how we understand the word "justice." Through the lens of a Western legal system, anyone is just who meets the standard of the law. But a Hebraic understanding of justice is more relational: anyone is just who keeps one's covenants and commitments to others.[27] Hence, we could say that God is considered just not because of meeting a standard that says a penalty is required, but because God is faithful to his covenantal promise to provide salvation to Israel and through Israel to the world.

It seems clear, then, that our interpretations of biblical texts on the atonement are dependent on and intertwined with our understanding of a number of other biblical and theological concepts, including sin, judgment, mercy, justice, and salvation, to name a few. This is all the more reason why, in a few pages, I cannot offer an adequate argument for or against any particular approach to the atonement. Hopefully, however, I have said enough to remind us that we can read even such key texts in multiple ways.

The Presentations of the Atonement in This Book

At the close of *Recovering the Scandal of the Cross*, we anticipated further work on the atonement:

> No one model of the atonement will fit all sizes and shapes, all needs and contexts where the church is growing and active in mission. This means, ultimately, that the next chapter of this book is being written in hundreds of places throughout the world, where communities of Jesus' disciples are practicing the craft of theologian-communicator and struggling with fresh and faithful images for broadcasting the mystery of Jesus' salvific death.[28]

The present book presents a number of these "next chapters." I have intentionally sought out contributions from different contexts, and my introduction to each chapter will locate the presentation in a place and time. At the end of each chapter I reflect theologically and missiologically on the atonement presentation in that chapter. In putting this book together, I did not seek presentations that used different images to communicate one particular explanation of the atonement. Rather, I sought out people, from a variety of theological backgrounds and contextual settings, who used stories and images to highlight different aspects of the saving significance of the cross and resurrection. Some explicitly use biblical texts in their presentations; others do not. All, however, are biblical in the sense that they are faithful to the apostolic message, as described in guidelines earlier in this chapter, and because, like the biblical writers, they seek both to connect with and to challenge their audience.

Although the book contains a diversity of presentations about the cross and resurrection, it does remain narrowly focused on the atonement. This focus does not, however, mean to imply that our preaching, teaching, and conversation about the cross and resurrection should be limited to the atonement. In fact, my hope is that the images of atonement in this book will help Christian communities see the relationship between the cross and resurrection and discipleship more easily than they do when they look at the cross through the lens of penal satisfaction. In reality, the gospel weaves many strands together at the cross: our salvation, a call to discipleship, an example to follow, pastoral comfort, hope, and so on. The strands cannot, and should not, be isolated from each other. This book focuses on the strand of salvation in the tapestry of the cross and resurrection, but other strands of the tapestry will also be evident in the presentations that follow.

I hope that the following chapters will be a catalyst to advance creative thinking about communicating the atonement today. I pray that this book will aid all readers in the task of articulating the saving significance of the cross and resurrection. I also pray that God's Spirit will use these presentations to give each reader a more profound awareness of the depth and breadth of the atoning work of the cross and resurrection in ways that will enrich, comfort, challenge, and lead to a response of praise and worship.

2

Deeper Magic
Conquers Death and the
Powers of Evil

C. S. LEWIS

What is sin? How does Satan rule and enslave? How does God provide salvation from sin and freedom from Satan's reign? Often stories help us understand answers to these questions in ways beyond what we can grasp from statements in a theology text. C. S. Lewis, a masterful story-teller, takes us to another world, Narnia, to help us better understand the power of sin and salvation in our world. Lewis wrote *The Lion, the Witch and the Wardrobe*, the first of *The Chronicles of Narnia*, in England in 1950. Lewis's story clearly displays the substitutionary character of Christ's death. However, unlike stories that paint a picture of penal substitution, Lewis does not portray Aslan as suffering a punishment from God that another person (in this case, Edmund) deserved. The conflict is with the Witch.

The story is meaningful in ways far beyond this brief summary! For instance, rather than describing Aslan's death as a payment to a Satan figure, one could also emphasize how Aslan suffers the consequences of sin that the human, Edmund, deserved to suffer. The theme of "deeper magic" and how that conquered the power of death and evil provides an opportunity for rich reflection.

In *The Lion, the Witch and the Wardrobe*, the four Pevensie children enter a wardrobe in World War II England and find themselves in Narnia, a world of talking animals. The feared and deceitful White Witch, a Satan figure, is ruling Narnia. Throughout the book Lewis graphically portrays her great power as well as the tragic and sad results of her rule. She has brought unending winter to Narnia and with her magic wand has turned those who resist her rule into stone statues. Edmund, one of the Pevensie children, came under the Witch's sway when she gave him delicious Turkish Delight; promised him more, and offered to make him a prince. He ate so much Turkish Delight he got sick, yet he craved more. The Witch used that craving to manipulate him. As Lewis's readers know, her goal was to keep Edmund and his brother and sisters from becoming royalty. The Witch's influence soured Edmund's relationship with his siblings and he deserted them, but all too soon found that life with the Witch was not what he imagined.

When Aslan, a great Lion and Christ figure, came to Narnia, he brought immediate change. The snow started melting and the animals tasted a freedom and joy they had not experienced under the White Witch. Although the Witch had hoped to use Edmund to entrap and kill all four children, with Aslan's arrival she decided to kill Edmund. Just before she sliced his throat, however, Edmund was rescued by animals loyal to Aslan. They brought Edmund to Aslan and he was reconciled with his brother and sisters and with Aslan.

The White Witch had not yet played her final card, however. Coming before Aslan, she protested that Edmund was a traitor and that according to the Deep Magic which the Emperor-beyond-the-sea (Lewis's God figure) had put into Narnia, all traitors belonged to her. She had the right to kill Edmund, she claimed. The newly reconciled children were aghast. Aslan walked away and talked privately with the White Witch and, unbeknownst to the children and the animals, Aslan offered to die in Edmund's place if she would renounce her claim on his life.

Later that day Susan and Lucy Pevensie accompanied a somber Aslan to the huge Stone Table, and then hidden in the bushes, watched in horror as Aslan allowed beasts loyal to the Witch to bind him, shave his mane, and muzzle him. They mocked him, spit on him and hit him, and then hoisted him on to the Stone Table. Lewis describes what happened next:

> The Witch bared her arms as she had bared them the previous night when it had been Edmund instead of Aslan. Then she began to whet her knife. It looked to the children, when the gleam of the torchlight fell on it, as if the knife were made of stone, not of steel, and it was a strange and evil shape.
>
> At last she drew near. She stood by Aslan's head. Her face was working and twitching with passion, but his looked up at the sky, still quiet, neither angry nor afraid, but a little sad. Then, just before she gave the blow, she stooped down and said in a quivering voice,
>
> "And now, who has won? Fool, did you think that by all this you would save the human traitor? Now I will kill you instead of him as our pact was, and so the Deep Magic will be appeased. But when you are dead, what will prevent me from killing him as well? And who will take him out of my hand *then*? Understand that you have given me Narnia forever, you have lost your own life, and you have not saved his. In that knowledge despair and die."
>
> The children did not see the actual moment of the killing. They couldn't bear to look and had covered their eyes.
>
> While the two girls still crouched in the bushes with their hands over their faces, they heard the voice of the Witch calling out,
>
> "Now! Follow me all and we will set about what remains of this war! It will not take us long to crush the human vermin and the traitors now that the great Fool, the great Cat, lies dead."[1]

After the Witch and her hoard of beasts left, the girls crept out and stroked Aslan's lifeless body and wept. They managed to remove the muzzle from his face but could not untie the cords holding his body to the Stone Table. They passed a sad and miserable night. As dawn approached and the sky began to lighten a very strange thing occurred. Many mice came, crawled on to the Table, and gnawed through the cords. The girls cleared away the remains of the cords and began walking around to get warm. Just as the sun broke the horizon they heard a great cracking noise. They turned around to see the Stone Table was broken in two and Aslan's body was gone.

> "Oh, oh, oh!" cried the two girls, rushing back to the Table.
> "Oh, it's *too* bad," sobbed Lucy; "they might have left the body alone."
> "Who's done it?" cried Susan. "What does it mean? Is it more magic?"
> "Yes!" said a great voice behind their backs. "It is more magic." They looked round. There shining in the sunrise, larger than they had seen him before, shaking his mane (for it had apparently grown again) stood Aslan himself.[2]

The girls, both frightened and glad, stammered through a conversation with Aslan trying to determine, without actually saying it, whether he was a ghost. They quickly decided he was real and hugged and kissed him.

> "But what does it all mean?" asked Susan when they were somewhat calmer.
> "It means," said Aslan, "that though the Witch knew the Deep Magic, there is a magic deeper still which she did not know. Her knowledge goes back only to the dawn of time. But if she could have looked a little further back, into the stillness and the darkness before Time dawned, she would have read there a different incantation. She would have known that when a willing victim who had committed no treachery was killed in a traitor's stead, the Table would crack and Death itself would start working backward."[3]

After romping playfully with the two girls Aslan stated they must turn to business. He let out a great roar and rushed off to the Witch's castle to release from their stone bondage all the creatures whom the Witch had turned to stone. Then all of them went to join the battle against the Witch and her forces who were surprised and quickly overwhelmed.

I begin the book with C. S. Lewis for a number of reasons. It is a gesture of honor and respect for this great thinker, who has gone before us. Chronologically, it is the oldest contribution. Like the following chapter, it reaches back to the church's earliest theological explanations of the atonement, which emphasize the cross and resurrection as a victory over death and the devil. So in these two chapters we return to our roots.

I also begin with Lewis because he does so well what I hope others will do. He develops a story, an image that does not simply repeat biblical phrases about the atonement, but helps his audience to understand and feel the reality of biblical atonement teaching. Like any metaphor or image, his tale does not communicate all there is to understand about the saving significance of the cross and resurrection. But as an image, a narrative, it communicates layers of meaning, more than would be possible in simply repeating an explanation of the atonement in propositional form.

Words Lewis wrote elsewhere apply not only to his work but are also important to keep in mind as you read other presentations in this book. In a short chapter in *Mere Christianity*, Lewis discusses the atonement. He offers an explanation and image of substitutionary atonement different from the one above, yet also different from traditional penal substitution. Lewis frames his explanation, or theory of the atonement, by emphasizing what is primary: Christ's death and resurrection put us right with God and gave us a fresh start. The theories and images we use to try to explain how that happens are secondary. He writes, "Such is my own way of looking at what Christians call the Atonement. But remember [that] this is only one more picture. Do not mistake it for the thing itself; and if it does not help you, drop it."[4]

3

Rising Victorious

Frederica Mathewes-Green

As a young adult Frederica Mathewes-Green became a Christian and about twenty years later joined the Eastern stream of Christianity, the Orthodox Church. The Orthodox Church has not embraced a penal satisfaction understanding of the atonement in the way that much of the Western church has. This contemporary example of an Orthodox presentation is directly related to the explanations and imagery of atonement developed by theologians in the second and third centuries, views of the atonement that proclaim the cross and resurrection as a victory over the devil and death. This presentation is excerpted from an article published in *Christianity and the Arts*, a periodical directed toward Protestant readers interested in the arts.[1]

Jesus is standing on the broken doors of hell. The massive portals lie crossed under his feet, a reminder of the cross that won this triumph. He stands braced and striding, like a superhero, using his mighty outstretched arms to lift a great weight. That weight is Adam and Eve themselves, our father and mother in the fallen flesh. Jesus grasps Adam's wrist with his right hand and Eve's with his left as he pulls them forcibly up, out of the carved marble boxes that are their graves. Eve is shocked and appears almost to recoil in shame, long gray hair streaming. Adam gazes at Christ with a look of stunned awe, face lined with weary age, his long tangled beard awry. Their limp hands lie in Jesus's powerful grip as he hauls them up into the light.

Behind Christ stand King David, King Solomon, the prophet Isaiah, and the prophet Jeremiah, all in gorgeous robes, clustered tightly like a standing-room-only crowd to see this marvelous event. Among them is an air of joy, even conviviality. John the Baptist is in the throng, still clothed in camel skin, now in full repossession of his head. Behind them are ranks and ranks of the righteous dead, who are dead no more, for Christ has set them free.

Beneath Christ's feet is a black receding pit with floating silver shards of metal, chains, locks, and ominous instruments of pain. These instruments are broken and shattered, and the locks are unhinged, except for one set, still intact and in use. These locks bind the body of that vicious old Satan, who grimaces in his captivity, bound hand and foot and cast into his own darkness.

When you consider images of the resurrection, what do you ponder? Probably not this traditional image used in the Eastern Orthodox Church. In the West, our first image is usually a graceful one: women who had been trudging toward the tomb on a misty Sunday dawn stand stock-still in astonishment. An angel is sitting on a round stone, with one hand raised in the air.

The image conveys a sense of silence and the stillness of caught breath as it reveals the moment on which the whole world turns. Colors are muted. The dew wets the hem of the women's dresses, and for a moment all is still. This garden-tomb image answers the question at the end of the three days, "Who rolled away the stone?" But there is another question, "Where did he go?"

"Did you not know that I must be about my Father's business?" Jesus might ask us once again. In Orthodoxy, we believe that the central meaning of the resurrection is victory. Thus, our traditional image is more vibrant and noisy, and it rings with a victorious shout. The resurrection is a victory over sin, death, and the devil, and a victory over the dark forces that enslave us, despise us, and wish to destroy us. Hence, we cry hundreds of times between Pascha (Easter) and Pentecost, "Christ is risen from the dead, trampling down death by death, and upon those in the tombs bestowing life!"

For long millennia, the righteous were trapped in the lair of Satan. "And all these, though well attested by their faith, did not receive what was promised, since God had foreseen something better for us, that apart from us they should not be made perfect" (Heb. 11:39–40 RSV). Even those who were not righteous heard the ringing voice of Christ in the grave: "For Christ also died for sins once for all, the righteous for the unrighteous, that he might bring us to God, being put to death in the flesh but made alive in the spirit, in which he went and preached to the spirits in prison, who formerly did not obey, when God's patience waited in the days of Noah" (1 Pet. 3:18–20 RSV). It was to the spirits in prison that Jesus went; he defeated that cruel jailer and set them free.

When we turn to the biblical story of the resurrection, we find that, in Matthew at least, it's not as silent as our imaginations suggest (28:1–10 RSV). As the women arrive at the tomb, there is "a great earthquake," caused by the descent of an angel. "His appearance was like lightning," an image that succeeds in astonishing because we cannot visualize what it means. He is dressed in robes white as snow, whiter than any fabric could be in that era.

The angel rolls away the stone and, in a closing gesture of command, sits upon it. That settles that. The terror-stricken guards, whose training had not covered this situation, are so frozen with fear that they "became as dead men." The women are not much less terrified, but they listen as the angel tells them not to be afraid. He gives them instructions: "Go and tell the disciples to meet Jesus in Galilee" (paraphrased).

As they depart "with fear and great joy," they meet the Lord himself, fresh from his triumph over death. As the women fall at his feet, he repeats the angel's message: "Go and tell my brethren to go to Galilee."

This version of the story differs from that in the Gospel of Mark, and that perplexing version is even more intriguing (16:1–8 RSV). As Mark has it, the women go to anoint Jesus's body, but instead find in the tomb "a young man sitting on the right side, dressed in a long white robe." He tells them that Jesus is risen and instructs them to tell the disciples. But here Mark tells us that they are terrified and flee the tomb. "And they said nothing to any one, for they were afraid." The earliest versions of this, the earliest Gospel, end abruptly at this point.

It's an odd gap between that small vignette of fear and retreat, and all that came next: the apostles' relentless courage unto death, not ascribable to mere fond memories of a really nice dead guy; the preaching of the gospel across the Mediterranean bowl; the persecutions and martyrdom; the establishment and rise of the church; and finally, the disintegration of Christendom in these present times, perhaps a prelude to full-circle persecution and martyrdom.

But at one mesmerizing moment, the news of Christ's resurrection was held by a handful of women who were too scared to tell anyone. But tell they did, and the story went on unreeling, till half a world away and two thousand years later it rings out with loud joy. Hundreds of times in the season of Pascha we will sing: "Christ is risen from the dead, trampling down death by death, and upon those in the tombs bestowing life!"

For those accustomed to hearing the atonement portrayed as a transaction in which Jesus's punishment on the cross satisfied God's requirement for justice, Mathewes-Green's graphic imagery of triumph and release is startling in its drama and celebration of victory. It easily leads one to want to join with others in shouting the words of praise, "Christ is risen from the dead...!" Yet her approach to proclaiming the saving significance of the cross and resurrection in terms of a triumph over Satan and the powers of sin and death is hardly new. The Gospels display Jesus in conflict with powers of evil throughout his ministry. Paul describes sin as an enslaving power (Rom. 6:12, 14, 23; 7:14). And in numerous places New Testament writers proclaim atonement while using a conflict-victory motif (e.g., Gal. 4:3–9; Eph. 1:19–22; 2:14–16; 3:7–13; 6:12; Phil. 2:9–11; Col. 1:13–14; 2:8–15; 1 Pet. 3:18–22). A *Christus Victor* model of the atonement was the most common explanation of the atonement for the first thousand years of the church.[2] Some early theologians' teaching on the *Christus Victor* model of the atonement included too much speculative detail on the mechanics of the victory (such as portraying God as using trickery to snare Satan, with Jesus as the bait). Mathewes-Green wisely avoids these extremes and offers a helpful model that others can adapt for use in their contexts.

4

Atonement
in the Coffee Shop

CHRIS FRIESEN

Most of the chapters in this book are from settings where people had the opportunity to give a well-developed presentation of the atonement. Many of our opportunities to proclaim the scandal of the cross, however, will come in comments we make during a group Bible study or in the midst of conversations—sharing ideas or responding to questions from both Christians and non-Christians. I hope that this book will not only aid readers in developing formal presentations of the atonement, but that they also will be able to adapt images from the book and use them in conversations. This chapter portrays that happening in a conversation between a member of a search committee and a woman he is interviewing.

Chris Friesen grapples with the meaning of atonement through the medium of a dramatic short story, an approach that demonstrates the crucial role of Christian imagination in contemplating and communicating the things of God. In wide-ranging conversation between the two lead characters, Friesen develops and tests images that communicate the saving significance of the cross in terms of stain and absorption, enmity and reconciliation, and the transformative potential of loving nonresistance. In his pastoral ministry at Lendrum Mennonite Brethren Church, Edmonton, Alberta, he has the privilege of engaging in vigorous theological discussion in local coffee shops and other venues. This fictional work is a fruit of those conversations. He preached a version of this dialogue in the summer of 2003. The audience he imagines for this presentation of ideas is himself and his peers, and also well-educated postevangelical skeptics torn between the conservatism of their upbringing and the assumptions of the professional, secular strata of society they inhabit.

If one extends imaginary lines back along one's thumb and forefinger, they meet and define a small triangle of skin at the edge of the hand. This is the area where we would have additional webbing if God had created us as water-dwelling creatures. It's also the place where I noticed a small tattoo when Aviva took off her cycling gloves.

It was a synesthetic revelation. Somebody was grinding something behind the front counter as she worked the crocheted fabric and worn leather off each finger. Then, the aroma of pulverized coffee beans that drifted over us as she reached out to shake my hand gave the impression that the mark on her skin had its own smell. It was not the kind of esoteric embellishment one is liable to glimpse in the small of a back or on the side of a foot, on summer days in the new millennium: it was no figure in any oriental script, not a butterfly, not a precise, gilded dragon. In fact, the edges of the stark image were already blurring, and the ink was taking on the hue of an old ballpoint pen—two brief intersecting lines proportioned as a cross. I decided I'd wait till later to ask her about it.

We bought our hot drinks and chatted about the weather, particularly as it related to her mode of transportation. The long-sleeved cotton knit she was wearing had darker blue sections on the arms and shoulders where moisture had seeped through her cycling jacket. She suggested that how a person looked at the rain made all the difference.

Aviva was the one to pry us out of small talk. "I have a question before we get started."

"Fire away."

"Is your church concerned mostly with a candidate's specific competencies, or are you looking for a leader with a certain image . . . or gender?"

I assured her that competence was paramount and that the only image requirement stipulated by the search committee was the image of God. She didn't blink. For good measure I added that there was no glass ceiling in our fellowship, only glass doors—but they were on hinges anyway.

"I'm happy to hear that," said Aviva. "I should also say from the start that I'm feeling a little apprehensive about creedal requirements. I tend to be on the blended side, doctrinally."

"Strathcona Christian Fellowship holds in creative tension a wide range of Christian outlooks," I recited, unintentionally quoting from our new church brochure.

"That sounds healthy," she responded, nodding. "Yet it's also important for a community of faith to hold on to some doctrinal distinctives, especially if it wants to live out an evangelical Christian identity."

"What would you consider some of those distinctives to be?" I asked, glad for an opportunity to get the questioning going in the direction it was supposed to be going, and a little unsettled by her use of the term "evangelical."

"The divinity of Christ, for example. A high view of the Scriptures. A robust understanding of atonement. Those are some good starting points."

The adult Sunday school class at our small university church flitted across my mind's eye. How would it hear this conversation? There was the fact of its ongoing protest against the Scripture-worship we labeled "fundamentalism," and there were also the painful questions a number of us had been voicing in the last year about how the traditional doctrine of penal substitution resembles the sacred violence generally employed in cultures of this world, in efforts to appease hungry and equally violent deities.

"Can you unpack those distinctives a little?" I asked, venturing a sip of my coffee. "Perhaps you can also say something about how you understand the adjective 'evangelical.'"

She hadn't missed a beat yet and didn't now either. "Walter Brueggemann's definition is my favorite. For him, evangelical

Christianity, in the truest sense of the word, is Christianity that 'mediates active rescue from our common deathliness.'"

"Could we consider coffee evangelical as well, in that case?"

Now she missed a beat, but only just.

"Uh, not without diluting the concept rather significantly. Some kinds of rescue are more superficial than others." I noticed the string of a teabag dangling a little square of green paper out of her mug.

"While we're into definitions," I said while trying to break a hard piece of biscotti in half, "I'd be interested in hearing your preferred explanation of atonement."

I managed to break the biscotti, but in the process knocked my hand against my mug and sloshed espresso onto the glass tabletop. "Drat." Aviva stepped over to a nearby table and brought back some napkins.

"Maybe I could try presenting it in three dimensions. Suppose this were Jesus," she said, standing a napkin at the edge of the table. "What would Jesus do?"

"Faced with a mess like this?"

"Yes."

"Jesus probably has more profound things to concern himself with than spilled espresso."

"Well, suppose this is something more profound than espresso," she said. "Suppose it represents everything that's wrong with the world. You know: things break, stuff gets spilled, people get burned."

I gasped. "Did I splash it on you too?"

"No, no, I'm just playing with the idea." She pulled a damp strand of hair back from her face and tucked it behind her ear. "Let's say this dark stuff represents the bitterness people carry inside because of everything that's wrong with the world. It's the poison of resentment, it's primal enmity—an instinctive, addictive hatred of each other and of God."

"Hey, go easy on coffee, will you?" I protested.

She politely ignored me. "So what would Jesus do?"

I wasn't having much luck getting hold of the horns of this conversation, but now I saw an opening for a little conceptual assertiveness of my own. "Would you mind if I played the part of God for a moment?"

"Not at all," said Aviva.

"Okay, how about this: Jesus knows that God hates mess, so what Jesus would do is put himself between the mess and God." I took the napkin from her, unfolded it, and held it in front of my eyes. "From now on, when God looks through Jesus—surprise, surprise—the world appears to be clean, even though it really isn't. In other words, atonement is a cover-up, an exercise in divine self-deception." Aviva listened with a calm, possibly even a warm, expression on her face. "Or maybe I should say, atonement is an exercise in distraction, since nothing in heaven or earth can be hidden from God, not even spilled coffee. Therefore, God needs to have his attention diverted from the everyday evil of the world by the worst evil of all—the sight of his own Son being unfolded and torn to pieces like a napkin. Once that happens, everything is peachy keen, because, contrary to the well-known proverb, two wrongs really do make a right."

A person who had just sat down at the table nearest us got up and moved to another one. I was a little surprised at the tone of my own voice. Aviva gazed at me for a moment, apparently gauging the measure of devilish advocacy in what I had just said.

"That may be truer than you think. Only, it would have to be two wrongs in the same direction, and the second one would have to be a wrong willingly and radically embraced by the one being wronged."

Now it was my turn to miss a beat.

"I don't follow you."

"Remember the Sermon on the Mount? 'You have heard that it was said, "Eye for eye, and tooth for tooth." But I tell you, Do not resist an evil person. If someone strikes you on the right cheek, turn to them the other also' [Matt. 5:38–39 NIV]."

"Go on."

"I think the basic idea here is that the other cheek—the second wrong—has the potential to shame the evil person into recognizing one's own self, especially when the one being struck chooses deliberately not to retaliate but instead to love the enemy with a steady, fearsome kind of love. Under such circumstances, the turning of the other cheek is a shocking revelation, a double revelation—of guilt on the one hand and of love on the other." Aviva could tell I was only partly catching on and continued her appeal with enthusiasm. "Don't you see? The pattern Jesus teaches in the Sermon on the Mount doesn't come out of nowhere. It's not like the human half of a divine double standard. On the contrary, it's a pattern anchored in God's own nature. Remember what Jesus says at the end of this teaching? 'Be perfect, therefore, *as your heavenly Father is perfect*' [Matt. 5:48 NIV, emphasis added]."

"Easy for him to say."

"Not at all. Don't forget that it's on the cross that Jesus finally practices what he preaches," said Aviva. "At that climactic moment, we see God himself turning the other cheek to humanity."

The ground under me seemed to shift slightly, and the hands of my mind jerked out to grab something and secure my balance.

"In what sense are you using the word 'God'? God the Father wasn't on the cross."

"Doesn't Paul say that all God's fullness dwelled in Jesus?"

"Paul's been known to be wrong before," I blurted, not really thinking through what I was saying. "In any case, it sounds like you're leaving atonement out of the picture now."

"No, I'm not," said Aviva. "This is the most profound kind of atonement of all. Atonement is at-one-ment—making one, restoring relationship where it has been destroyed. And that's just what the love of the one turning the other cheek is seeking to accomplish. God could have taken eye for eye and tooth for tooth. But instead of swatting us like mosquitoes or stretching his skin taut around the place where we were pricking him so that we simply exploded with his blood, God patiently let us do our worst to him, thereby gaining a way to change us that doesn't require destroying us."

Someone was releasing pressurized steam into liquid in a metal cup at the front.

"So God's way of changing us involves us flying off with God's blood in our bellies?" I asked.

"Wow," she said. "Now there's a eucharistic image. Not particularly equitable, however, since it only applies to the female mosquito."

The subject of mosquitoes got me thinking about needles going into skin. I started formulating a segue to the topic of Aviva's tattoo but discovered that she wasn't finished reasoning with me yet.

"We're probably mixing our metaphors a little too freely here," she said. "Getting back to our earlier symbol of coffee, I think we could say that, on the cross, God let human beings pour out all their bitterness on him, let them spend their wrath on him, if you will, and in the process disclosed what all human beings really are—those at war with the One who loves them. Once the cross truly reveals this to us, we lay down our weapons, weeping, and enter his embrace, so vividly represented in Christ's spread-eagled arms. God has made peace with us. Not us with God, but God with us."

"It's an attractive idea, Aviva. Now do you think you can show it to me in the New Testament?"

"Do you have a Bible with you?"

While she flipped through the dog-eared copy I happened to have in my briefcase, I drank some more coffee. Was it my imagination, or was it acquiring something of a sour aftertaste as it cooled off? I wondered if I was going to get a chance to deal with the more practical question of Aviva's ministry experience.

She began to read aloud: "This is from Colossians 1 [vv. 19–20 NIV]: 'For God was pleased to have all his fullness dwell in him, and through him to reconcile to himself all things, whether things on earth or things in heaven, by making peace through his blood, shed on the cross.' So it's God making the peace. And it's God reconciling all things to himself, not reconciling himself to all things, as if God were the one who needed to change his attitude or get distracted or cover up the facts. Listen to this: 'Once you were alienated from God and were enemies in your minds because of your evil behavior. But now he has reconciled you by Christ's physical body through death to present you holy in his sight, without blemish and free from accusation' [vv. 21–22 NIV]."

"'Free from accusation,'" I repeated. "I didn't hear anybody getting accused of anything in your model. Once you start talking about accusation, we're back at the first model I presented, the one where something needs to happen to convince God to stop accusing us, something that can make us 'holy in his sight.' Not holy for real, mind you, just holy 'in his sight.'"

"How could there be any difference between the two?" Aviva asked. "What God sees is what is real, and what is real, God sees."

"Well, in that case I guess there's no hope for thoroughgoing coffee addicts like myself. God will have to accuse us forever."

"It isn't God that we designate with the name Accuser," she said quietly.

"Right."

We had the first significant gap in our conversation. Aviva shifted in her seat, and I watched a man who looked like a street person walk into the café and sit down without buying anything. He seemed agitated. I was just drawing a breath to move the discussion in a new direction when Aviva continued.

"I think the language of freedom from accusation comes into the argument for the benefit of our weak human consciences."

"You think so?" I was feeling in my briefcase for my notebook but couldn't seem to locate it.

"Yes," she said. "Once relationship has been restored, it's terribly important for us to know that our striking of the cheek isn't being held against us—that the assault has been plainly and wholly absorbed. Typically, we need some word or sign to convince us. Thus, for example, Jesus announces to the paralyzed man, without even being asked to do so, 'Son, your sins are forgiven' [Mark 9:2 NRSV]. This is the same kind of reassurance that the sign of blood used to give—and still does. Blood, you see, is for the sinner's benefit, not God's. Even the book of Hebrews sees it like that."

"*Even* the book of Hebrews?" I raised my eyebrows.

"What I mean is that if any New Testament document would have been liable to get tangled up in the logic of using blood as currency in the purchase of forgiveness, it would have been Hebrews. But even Hebrews connects the sign of blood with a human need." She began to flip pages in my Bible again. "As if God would have to see blood before God would do anything merciful! Where does that come from?"

"Maybe there's something in the water," I offered, "or . . . in the coffee."

"Touché!" She smiled. "It *is* the second most commonly traded commodity in the world, you know."

"What's the first?"

"Crude oil."

Aviva soon found what she was looking for. "Now, who is the one who needs the persuasion of blood? Is it God? I don't think so. 'How much more, then, will the blood of Christ . . . cleanse our consciences from useless rituals?'—'useless rituals' is the footnote reading, by the way—'so that we may serve the living God!' [Heb. 9:14 NIV]. In other words, 'You're forgiven, people, so get over it already.' Then in the next chapter it says, 'Therefore, . . . since we have confidence'—finally—'to enter the Most Holy Place by the blood of Jesus, . . . let us draw near to God with a sincere heart in full assurance of faith, having our hearts sprinkled to cleanse us from a guilty conscience' [10:19, 22 NIV]."

"Does that mean 'sprinkled with blood'?"

"That's the allusion. And, getting back to your question about the Colossians passage, it all serves to remind us that, since Christ turned the other cheek, praying for forgiveness even while we executed him, no one has to accuse us anymore, not other people, not evil powers, not even ourselves. Yes, we surely have done evil in lashing out at God and each other, but when all is said and done, what does it matter? We are loved. The blood is the sign of both truths, especially the second."

"Meanwhile, back in the real world the tangible consequences of evildoing remain in force."

"How so?" she asked.

"Look at the table," I said. "All our theologizing hasn't managed to clean up this puddle of coffee yet." We both looked at it. "Perhaps you'd like to resume your original demonstration."

"I could do that."

"Here." I held up the napkin. "But before you proceed, I'd like to point out that, up to now, we seem merely to have taken Jesus from in front of God's eyes and placed him in front of our own. Unless I've missed something."

"We're the ones who need help for interpreting the world," Aviva said. "Why shouldn't we look through Jesus?"

"Anyway, I should let you finish your object lesson. Just make sure you explain it step by step as you go, so I can keep up with you." I handed her the napkin, and as she refolded it I took a rather arduous bite of the offending biscotti. "Jeez, if 'tooth for tooth' were still in effect, these guys would be in trouble." Aviva waited. "Please—go on."

"Okay," she said, "remember what this puddle represents: a bitter enmity spilled out in the world."

"Can I ask a question?"

"Already?"

"How did this get into the world in the first place?"

"That's a separate issue."

"I don't think it is. I mean, who brewed the coffee in the first place, and who put it in such a spillable cup? If enmity is simply inherent to being human and free-willed, as it seems to be, then how can God hold us fully responsible for it?"

"Whether God can or can't," she said, "God *doesn't* hold us fully responsible for it. God has gladly taken responsibility for it himself." She held up the napkin. "Earlier I said that this is Jesus. Jesus, then, is God the Father entering the mess"—she moved the napkin as if it were a human figure—"embracing the enmity and suffering and guilt and death of the world from the inside and absorbing it into himself. It's the same kind of absorption as turning the other cheek, but now on a cosmic scale." She dropped the napkin into the middle of the puddle, which was wider than it. In a moment, the white paper turned brown.

"Your God is too small."

"Well, yes; then let's bear in mind the trinitarian nature of the work and use three napkins," said Aviva. She added two more on either side of the first.

At that moment a verse popped into my head, giving me opportunity to show that, even though I was a middle-aged community college instructor rather than a fresh young seminarian like herself, I still knew my way around the Bible. I pointed at the first napkin: "'God made him who had no sin to be sin for us' [2 Cor. 5:21 NIV]?"

"Indeed," she said.

Then I wiped up the spill and held up the damp brown wad of napkins. "What happens to the stain now? If 'the Lamb of God . . . takes away the sin of the world' [John 1:29 NRSV], where does he take it to? Hell? It has to go somewhere."

"Every analogy limps," said Aviva. "Jesus has properties unknown to a napkin. Mysteriously, the bitterness disappears into him, or into his suffering, and God is still God, perfect and unstained."

"Sounds like Jesus is a kind of white hole that attracts rays of darkness and swallows them."

"Yes! Or maybe he's like a tiny seed of light that darkness tries to swallow, not understanding what it is, and then when he dies and turns into a supernova, he annihilates the darkness from within. That's the effect of resurrection."

I pondered that for a moment. "Not bad. Although you'll have to admit we've left the concrete world behind again."

"We have?"

"Well, if we haven't, we've certainly managed to cover it with some deep water. And I'm getting tired of keeping my arms and legs moving and my chin up. God means for human beings to live on dry ground. If it were otherwise, we would have webbed fingers and gills."

"Beavers don't have gills."

"Every analogy limps."

"Fair enough," she said. "But beavers are actually a really good analogy. Think of the way they try to contain and control water in order to make an environment suitable for their daily life. That's just like the work we're doing with language. We're trying to build dams around truth. We're trying to accumulate a reasonably still pool of truth in which to carry on the business of living."

"Business of living? Don't beavers spend just about all their time maintaining their dams, struggling to keep the water level right where they want it?"

"I don't know. They have to eat, too. They raise young—"

"Here's my point," I said. "If human beavers are going to spend the better part of their lives in coffee shops or churches or schools or wherever, building up words and ideas into great theological embankments that keep 'truth' at a level comfortable for them, then not much of anything useful is ever going to get done in this world."

"You'd prefer beavers to be less self-absorbed, more altruistic?"

"Yes, I would, now that you mention it! Now there's your cue to remind me that 'every analogy limps,'" I said, with a little more bite than intended.

"I'm just trying to understand your objection to the labor of theology."

"It's like this, Aviva: You obviously have a lot of creative ways of looking at reality—and don't get me wrong; I find many of them refreshing—but how does all this sophisticated religious subjectivity touch the everyday experience of the people around us, the people in this coffee shop, for instance? In the end, what difference does it make to them whether the cross is a sacrifice to appease God's wrath or a peace offering to appease human wrath or even some magic trick that turns evil into good? Has the world actually changed? It's as if we've been wiping the top of the table up in some Platonic heaven, and all along the coffee was on the underside of the glass. Mind you, in the real world, we're not talking about a little splash of espresso; we're talking about a flood of bitterness and evil, which is knee-deep at its lowest point. Coffee can't even come near to representing it. We're talking crude oil, Aviva, barrels and barrels of it, poured into the ocean and combusted into the atmosphere and set on fire as we blow each other up trying to monopolize it. Try believing your way out of that!"

"I don't have to believe my way out of it."

"For crying out loud, we're talking about a world in which turning the other cheek is an invitation to get your head knocked off! And all the while I'm supposed to convince myself by raw force of imagination that, despite appearances to the contrary, God actually loves us and has been taking care of business all along."

She looked at me intently. "Keith, don't you believe that there is objective, observable change in the earthly realm, right now, because of Jesus's death and resurrection?"

I returned her gaze silently. I had been giving full play to a skeptical mind in this conversation, having early on sensed a permission to do so. Now she was challenging me to make a decision.

"Let me make the question more concrete," she said. "Hasn't there been objective, observable change in your own life since you became a Christian?"

I had had vague misgivings that it might come to something like this. I took a deep breath. "When did I become a Christian?"

Aviva blinked. "When you began to release your stain to Christ for the first time, accepting the peace made by God. When you first gave up, in the name of Christ, a grievance against another person, because you had come to see that Christ has suffered under the weight of all grievance. When you yourself first absorbed some little portion of this world's bitterness and enmity through the power of Christ, having determined to follow the way of his cross, which leads to resurrection."

"When did *you* become a Christian?" I said, in what was nearly a whisper.

"I became a Christian on the same day that a village grandmother in Orissa, India, put this mark on my hand, eleven years ago," she said. She put her hand in the middle of the table, the same place where the puddle of espresso had been.

Finally given permission, I looked at the little cross freely. "She had a tattoo machine?"

Aviva shook her head. "Needles and dye."

"Did it hurt? I guess that's a stupid question."

"It wept for three days. Infected." Abruptly, Aviva's face creased sharply. It looked like she was holding her breath. Then she began to cry.

"I'm sorry; I shouldn't have brought it up."

Tears were running down her cheeks. "I'm not crying because of how it felt; I'm crying because the woman who gave it to me has now died."

"Oh. I'm sorry, Aviva."

Her eyes closed and the sides of her mouth convulsed. "Christ is marked on me, and I am marked on Christ." She put her forehead down on the table, on top of her hand.

With my own eyes blurring, I glanced around the café. The man who looked like a street person was the only one who seemed to have noticed our situation. He was watching us closely, in fact, almost glaring. Nevertheless, it didn't seem inappropriate to reach across the small table and put my hand on Aviva's shoulder briefly. In a short time, she became still and dried her eyes on the sleeve of her shirt.

Smiling faintly, and with a jerky breath, she said, "Anyone watching this interview would think you had been terribly hard on me."

"Maybe they'd be right," I said contritely. "I never even got to my easy questions. Will you help me finish these?" I passed her the small plate of biscotti. She took one, held it in her tea for a few seconds, still settling her breathing, then bit it cleanly in half. Nothing spilled. I gazed at the table with a bemused smile. "Getting to the matter of your specific competencies . . ."

"Looks like we may need to do a second round sometime, huh?"

"Well, yes, I was just going to say that considering the comprehensiveness of your résumé, we could probably leave the discussion of your ministry experience till the interview with the search committee and the board. I'm prepared to recommend you to that next step."

"Really?" She glanced away. Soon after that, the gears of her mind seemed to engage and accelerate, while something like astonishment began to creep over her face. "I don't mean to change the subject, Keith, but I think I've just realized why that man over there looks so familiar. I knew him in Yellowknife. He actually broke into my house on several occasions. Will you excuse me for just a moment? I haven't seen him for a long time, and I've got to say hi before he leaves."

She got up and walked over to the table where the man with the scruffy hair and kangaroo jacket was sitting. By the look on his face, he clearly recognized her. His age was difficult to judge: late forties? midfifties? Some gray in his black hair. Sharp cheeks and nose. They exchanged greetings, and he asked a question, indicating me with a frown. She laughed and shook her head, then explained something that I couldn't hear, pointing at me once. He nodded and responded, mostly in monosyllables. The conversation went on for a minute or two, and Aviva returned.

"I'm really sorry about this, but it looks as though I need to leave right now. Walter's having an anxiety attack and wants me to go with him to the clinic. I haven't seen him for five years. It's almost too incredible that we would bump into each other today." The man was already getting up and heading for the door. "I enjoyed this conversation, Keith. It would be great to continue it. And I'll get the tab next time."

"Even if I order coffee?"

"Absolutely."

We shook hands hurriedly.

"God bless, Aviva," I said, wishing to say more, but needing to say at least that.

"You too."

The rain had stopped. I watched her unlock her bike outside the front window and walk down 82nd Avenue beside Walter. Then I checked the calls on my cell phone. Two from Janet. I phoned immediately.

"Hi. How's it going? Yes, I'm finished now. Yes, really great. . . . Uh, by the way, I wanted to apologize for what I said this morning. No, I had no right to say that. It was my fault, actually. Okay. Yes. Yes, I should be home soon."

———

Friesen has presented us with two images of atonement: a napkin absorbing the stain of sin, and turning the other cheek. The medium of a dramatic encounter between fictional characters allows him to probe and explain those images in significant depth and in an engaging manner. Central to his explanation of the atonement is the system of algebraic justice that expects and requires a struck person to strike back and balance the relational equation. Rather than responding with the expected "response A" (striking back), however, God uses what we might call "the deeper math" (partially borrowing from C. S. Lewis), in which the substitution of "response B" (turning the other cheek) causes the algebraic justice itself to unravel, leading to a relational situation with remarkable possibilities for reconciliation and growth. God in Jesus loves those striking him to the degree that God "turns the other cheek," and in that act of suffering God reveals truth and wins relationship rather than potentially hardening the other by retribution and retaliation.

Aviva's image of the napkin absorbing spilled coffee moves in several directions. To begin with, it illustrates God's concrete rather than "virtual" engagement of the problem of sin/evil/stain, answering our sense that "something needs to be done here!" It implies that God in Jesus actually swallows the sin (cf. Paul's language in 1 Cor. 15:54 and 2 Cor. 5:4). Next, the napkin points to the absorption inherent in God's act of "turning the other cheek" on the cross, a model of atonement that emphasizes the person-to-person relational dynamics of Christ's self-sacrificial confrontation with evil and evildoers. That is, the encounter in which Christ the victim absorbs the striking of humankind has the potential to arouse the sinner to utterly repudiate his sin, though sin's effect remains in view in the form of the bruised cheek of the forgiving one. Friesen characterizes the absorption of both napkin and cheek as ultimately redemptive rather than destructive in intent. The humans are not wiped away with the stain.

Love spins out of the event in all directions. Through having Keith question the pragmatic portent of all this, Friesen is able to highlight the connection between God's substituting absorption for retribution (response B for response A) and our doing the same. Aviva speaks of Christians "[absorbing] some little portion of this world's bitterness and enmity through the power of Christ." Jesus is substituted in place of all the enemies we wish to punish. Once that occurs, even in imagination, and we see what our desire for vengeance has done and still does to Jesus, we are moved to drop the charges against the people around us. We realize that there is forgiveness for them as there is forgiveness for us. Through Jesus the power of "eye for eye, tooth for tooth," the algebraic equation of revenge, is broken decisively, thus introducing a new pattern for human relationships into the world, like putting yeast into a mass of dough.

At the story's end Friesen gives brief illustrations of the transformative potential of God's scandalous work of loving nonresistance on the cross. We see how Aviva's response of loving action rather than revenge and retaliation, to someone who wronged her in the past, has led to a certain at-one-ment. And we hear Keith apologizing to his wife rather than taking a combative stance and intensifying a conflict between them.

Chris Friesen suggested to me that I might invite readers to reflect on ways that Aviva's tattoo is integrated into this proclamation of the scandal of the cross. As an image it is not developed, but it remains in the background, inviting further thought—a "stain" that does not disappear, a wound that can turn into something beautiful. With that in mind, a second reading of the story may yield new insights. In that sense the story serves as a metaphor for the cross at another level as well. In the face of all of the explanations of the saving significance of the cross, there is a "surplus of meaning" in the cross and resurrection that invites ongoing theological interpretation and contextual practice.

5

A Different Story

Mark 15:21–39

Debbie Blue

This book aims to present various images of atonement through contextualizing some of the rich diversity of atonement teaching in the Bible. Unfortunately, many of us have read the Bible through the lens of penal satisfaction theory for so long that the biblical teaching on the atonement has become one-dimensional. Exposure to the insights of others can aid in seeing exciting textures in the biblical writings, ones that were always present but unseen because of the lens in use. René Girard has helped many to encounter new currents of meaning in the biblical text. His research and reflection on conflict, violence, victimization, and scapegoating in human cultures has provided fertile ground for thinking about the atonement.[1]

In this sermon Debbie Blue does a masterful job of using experiences of daily life to communicate some central elements of Girard's thought. She builds on those same stories to illuminate the biblical text and powerfully proclaim an aspect of the saving work of the cross and resurrection. Blue lives in community with family and friends in rural Minnesota. She is on the pastoral team at the House of Mercy in St.

Paul, where she preached this sermon in April 2003. It is a church that describes itself as offering a discriminating blend of high church and low church, of tradition and innovation, sincere worship and healthy skepticism.

And they compelled a passer-by, Simon of Cyrene, who was coming in from the country, the father of Alexander and Rufus, to carry his cross. And they brought him to the place called Golgotha (which means the place of a skull). And they offered him wine mingled with myrrh; but he did not take it. And they crucified him, and divided his garments among them, casting lots for them, to decide what each should take. And it was the third hour, when they crucified him. And the inscription of the charge against him read, "The King of the Jews." And with him they crucified two robbers, one on his right and one on his left. And those who passed by derided him, wagging their heads, and saying, "Aha! You who would destroy the temple and build it in three days, save yourself, and come down from the cross!" So also the chief priests mocked him to one another with the scribes, saying, "He saved others; he cannot save himself. Let the Christ, the King of Israel, come down now from the cross, that we may see and believe." Those who were crucified with him also reviled him. And when the sixth hour had come, there was darkness over the whole land until the ninth hour. And at the ninth hour Jesus cried with a loud voice, "Eloi, Eloi, lama sabachthani?" which means, "My God, my God, why hast thou forsaken me?" And some of the bystanders hearing it said, "Behold, he is calling Elijah." And one ran and, filling a sponge full of vinegar, put it on a reed and gave it to him to drink, saying, "Wait, let us see whether Elijah will come to take him down." And Jesus uttered a loud cry, and breathed his last. And the curtain of the temple was torn in two, from top to bottom. And when the centurion, who stood facing him, saw that he thus breathed his last, he said, "Truly this man was the Son of God!" (Mark 15:21–39 RSV)

There's a story I think you'll be familiar with. Sometimes it seems like it's the *only* story. You hear it over and over and see it over and over and tell it and make it and do it over and over. There are a jillion versions. Sometimes it seems big and destructive. Sometimes it seems little and good or even big and good. It just depends on who's telling it and how, and your relationship with the person telling it, whether or not they're on your side.

The story is "The Good Guys versus the Bad Guys," or in a slight variation, "United against Evil." It's a familiar story, right? I could tell a thousand versions, and I think I (or someone, anyway) could tell enough of the right versions to show that it's the story that's formed every civilization from the beginning of time. But I'll just tell three.

So, my husband, Jim, and I are on a date. A week earlier we arranged a babysitter because this was going to be our night out. We're driving out, down the driveway, and you can tell it isn't going to be such a good date. We have nothing to say. It's a long driveway. It is as though we hardly even want to be together. We can't quite get over earlier tension we had about stupid stuff: who empties the dishwasher more, who never ever ever thinks to clean out the refrigerator or sort through the clothes in the kids' drawers, but who remembers to change the oil in the car, and who tries to control the world, who does more, who's a better person?

It seems as though it might be a noncommunicative wasted babysitter night, when some guy in a huge monster pickup truck thing, with enormous wheels and a gun rack in the back and black mud flaps with a chrome silhouette of a naked woman, zooms past us on our little country gravel road, throwing up dust and rocks. He has what looks like a three-year-old kid up in the front, not only with no car seat but also no seat belt, *and* the man is smoking with the window shut. And every bumper sticker on his car is the opposite of every bumper sticker on our car (well, we have only one, but if we had more, they'd be the opposite of his).

We're like, whoa Mr. Country Dude, jeez. He so offends us. He practically runs us off the road (or maybe he just passes us fast), but he is certainly reckless, not only in driving, but also with his kid. We suddenly have so much to say about this. And as we keep driving, Jim says a couple of funny things about the man's offensiveness, which makes us laugh, and this reminds us of other funny things about some of the stereotypically rural attitudes of our neighbors. As it turns out, this guy saves our evening together. Whatever silly little things were making us feel separate or bad about ourselves or our relationship, in the face of this "other," we feel good and close and united.

Here's another version, rural again. There are Hoglunds that live all around us. I don't know if they are related or not. I think some are, some aren't. But the guy who sold us our farm warned us when we bought the place that there was a feud brewing between the Hoglunds on the south side of the road and the Hoglunds on the north side.

The northern Hoglunds, mostly by chance and the fact that their soil is a little better and they own really good cows, have a rather successful farm. The southern Hoglunds? Not so successful, in fact, not at all. They are doing so poorly that acre by acre they have sold off all their land to the northerners. Now Mr. Hoglund works at Hardware Hanks, and Mrs. Hoglund is a cashier at Little Dukes.

The northern Hoglunds' farming success has not made them popular in the neighborhood. There's an underlying rivalry, if you've never noticed, between people doing the same thing or people period, no matter who they are or what they do. Rivalry, rivalry, rivalry. We have heard stories. I don't know if it is true or not, but we have heard that one of the Hoglunds shot the other's dogs, and one dumped a load of manure right next to the other's house. I don't know if you're familiar with flies and manure and the country, but I can tell you, that house must have seemed like it was cursed by a plague. The Hoglund clan was deteriorating. There were rumors circulating about what might happen next.

Then we moved in. Right between them, four families from the cities, with little foreign cars and master's degrees and initially not a single pickup. We didn't know that you weren't supposed to drive down your driveway when the mud came. We got stuck a lot. We asked about what pesticides they were using and if the liquor store could maybe start carrying a "better beer," and we looked ridiculous and stupid to our neighbors.

One day Mr. South Hoglund and Mr. North Hoglund meet by chance at the Milaca Off-Sale and have the first laugh they've had together in years about these people who will pay seven dollars for a six-pack. And before long they are having barbecues and their dogs are running back and forth freely, and it has become clear that the problems in rural Minnesota are the fault of the city and its spreading influence. Us.

Okay, one more version. Are you at all familiar with second-grade girls? It almost seems as though they don't know how to be friends unless it's on the basis of excluding someone else for any arbitrary reason: they have bangs or pink pants or their name starts with the wrong letter. It's a ritual they reenact daily.

Works like a charm, this mechanism we have as humans. It's not just a little thing that pops up now and then. It's more like the basis on which we create our social order. It's like an anthropological fact: we construct our unity over against someone or some group or some other. We construct, we know, our goodness over against some other person or philosophy or way of being. How can we feel good or know good if we don't know what out there is bad, or define ourselves over against it? And it works better if there's a bad that seems "out there," something we think we are not really a part of (corporate America, fundamentalism, decadent living, worldliness, repressive government, whatever).

Like I said, you could tell a thousand versions of this story. Think about them. Some are unbelievably terrible and violent. But the point isn't to say, "Look how bad we are, or they are." It's like, "Look, isn't it true that this is what we do?" It's almost as though we can't get *out* of doing it. As though we're stuck. As though we don't know how else to be in the world, how else to make community or be unified unless it's over against something or someone or some group, or some other people's way of being in the world. We don't know how to feel good about ourselves unless we define our goodness over against someone else's badness or just lesserness (if we're not using moral categories, we might imagine that *they* are unfortunately just less enlightened). Maybe it's inevitable, this mechanism, over against, but it's not really harmless.

And the other part? It's really sort of a lie. Not just sort of a lie: it's always a lie. No matter who's telling it, white supremacists, Fascist dictators, fundamentalists, liberals, the Vote to Impeach Bush Campaign, peace activists, the people cheering when the statue of Saddam Hussein comes down, the people cheering when an effigy of Bush is burned. When you think, "It seems to me that the world really might be better, a less evil place, a safer place, if we got rid of certain people" (maybe you don't think we should kill them, but you definitely think *we* would be better off without *them*)—it's a lie. But, boy, don't we believe it. Almost more than we believe anything else. I mean, I can hardly say "It's a lie" right now, because I believe it so much (though I believe the story only if it's from my perspective or my community's perspective).

So, is that all there is? Just this same story from a thousand perspectives? Is there any other story, or is this really it, the definitive story? We can't create unity, community. We can't construct goodness except by defining it over against something "other." And if sometimes that leads to murderous violence, well, it's unfortunate, but I'm sorry, there's no other way. There's just no other way to be human in the world. It's in our genes, partner. It's the only story. That's it.

People have tended to use the story of Jesus dying on the cross as though it's the same story. As though Jesus is all concerned about promoting his good way against the bad religious leaders' way, or the Roman Empire's way, or the way of the powerful or the pagan or the fallen or the faithless. As though it is the ultimate over-against way. As though it's all about Jesus asking, "Are you with me [and by implication against the rest]?" As though he's offering us the opportunity to form the most important community, unified together in righteousness and belief in opposition to unbelief and faithlessness, and oh, how we must gather together to assure victory for this side, the right side, God's side. Really, it's just the same old, tired old, divisive, violent mechanism kicking in; the same story, just on a grander scale.

But I don't know; I mean, read the story in Mark. Jesus could have unified the crowd so easily against the religious leaders or the Romans. The crowd was predisposed to unify against them: the people, the poor and the weak, against the powerful and the privileged. Or the Jews against the Romans. Or the followers of Christ against the faithless. But this really isn't that story. It's not the story of God unifying God's people against an *other*. It's the story of all the people, the strong and the weak and the good and the bad, the religious and the pagans, all the people, everyone unifying against Jesus Christ, the incarnation of God's love in the world.

Mark takes pains in his story to make it clear (almost systematically) that it is everyone, the most unlikely allies: the chief priests and the scribes and the Roman soldiers and even the disciples and even the two criminals being crucified with him—all conspire at some level in the crucifixion of Jesus. And just in case that doesn't quite cover everybody, Mark's going to cover all the possibilities by mentioning that anybody who just happens to be passing by mocks him. They betray or mock him or seek his death, maybe to reinforce their system of righteousness, their goodness, or maybe to protect themselves, their sense of dignity or strength, at some level to keep themselves from being vulnerable. From this end, it looks as though the scapegoating machine is running full on, smooth and strong.

But Jesus in his death and resurrection does the farthest thing from oiling the wheels of that machine. He breaks it to pieces. He becomes the scapegoat for everyone to define themselves over against; he becomes utterly vulnerable to all of them, all of us. Jesus refuses to be *against* anything in this crucifixion scene. But is he just really making the biggest *against-us* move he could possibly make? Is he like the peace activist kind of thing, the go-limp kind of a thing, where protesters are completely nonviolent even though the police are handling them roughly? Where by refusing to be against, one makes the loudest and most powerful statement *against* that one can: against those who choose violence, against those people's way, against police officers or warmongers?

Or could it be that Jesus, the incarnation of God's love in the world, really isn't against? Doesn't come against anyone, but comes for us all? To get us? To scoop us up out of the death-dealing, death-making repetitious monotony of the machine, and into the love of God? Could it be that he comes thoroughly and honestly for the religious leaders? For the Romans? For the crowds? For the warriors? For the peace activists? For the urban? For the rural? For George and for Saddam and for the guy who smokes with his windows up? For the world, really the world? Could it be because God actually, really, thoroughly loves the world, likes it, and desires to be with it, even what deeply offends us ourselves? Could it be that God comes not out of a need to condemn someone, or a need to protect God's own strength, not out of a need to prove somehow God's invulnerability, but rather out of a desire to be in relationship with us, a need to free us all from the tired, false story we use to construct our nations, communities, religion, so that we might come into the love? This story isn't "The Bad Guys versus the Good Guys"; it isn't "United against Evil." It's the story of God's love.

The death and resurrection of Jesus Christ isn't a New Great Big Way to make the machine run, the Most Powerful Fuel Ever for that old mechanism, so that now God's people can clearly unify, the believers in Jesus against the unbelievers. It collapses the machine. The people may have used the machine over and over to claim some sort of divine goodness and righteousness, but this story reveals how all the people, everyone, use it to kill God. This narrative is not the ultimate reinforcement of being over against; instead, it reveals to us the destructiveness, futility, utter deathliness of all our againstness; it shows us how our deeply ingrained mechanism for creating unity leads to death, even the death of God.

But surprisingly, stunningly, beautifully, unexpectedly, and amazingly, the revelation does not end with utter condemnation for the violence at the heart of the social order. It doesn't finally reveal that all of "them," all of "us," are condemned for being such relentless and horrible scapegoaters, such pathetic people locked in endless rivalry. It's a story about Jesus absorbing, taking in, all our againstness, accepting all the death we have to hand out, all the fears that make it so impossible for us to be truly vulnerable, all the weakness that makes us mean. He takes it all totally and thoroughly in. And comes back. Comes back unbelievably undefeated by it. Comes back, not vengeful and resentful, all hyped to form some oppositional unity, some group communion against us (or anyone), all ready to get his army up against the bad, stupid scapegoating people. He comes back, and he comes back again and again and always, irrepressibly for them, us, all. He comes back loving and forgiving and desiring, as always, communion with the world.

It's a little hard to grasp. It may not even seem entirely appealing to us, but the Gospel doesn't tell this story to harden our hearts against anyone. It's given to us to break our hearts open. To make love and communion. To make relationship with the Other (who's the complete other) possible. To reveal to us how we are all together now, not in opposition, not in condemnation, but in forgiveness, gathered together in the love of God.

It doesn't seem like this story should fuel our sense of divine righteousness against bad people, wrong ways, strange, weird others; it seems like it might break our hearts open, for relationship based not on exclusion but on the ridiculously inclusive forgiving and redeeming love of God. It shows us that we can't relieve our separateness by making a scapegoat; we can't create love and unity fueled by againstness. The old mechanism, the old story, is not creative of communion; or if it is, that love and communion is some thin, false, scared union compared to the new, practically unimaginable, vitally alive, thorough, and wild communion made possible by the love and grace of God.

Jesus dies, not to convict us for our crime, but to scoop us up for life lived and fed by a whole different fuel, something completely other than rivalry, scapegoating, vengeance, and violence. We are freed by the love and the grace of God not to get our identity, manufacture our love, our community, our unity, by defining ourselves over against the bad, the country, the city, Republicans, liberals, Britney Spears, George Bush, or Saddam Hussein. Instead, we can get our identity, love, community, unity from the revelation that I or you or George or Saddam actually stand together (I know this is offensive), condemned and forgiven, loved and sought after, desired by God. We are freed to form our identities, love, communion, unity from the love that is resolutely not based on drawing lines between parties, but on breaking down the most impenetrable lines. It frees us not to play out the old script over and over and over always. Can you see how this might work? We are free to form community, drawn and transformed by this new story, not the old death-dealing, death-making story.

I know I am not done being transformed, because when I think of what really often does seem to work to make me feel good and loved and in communion, it's the guy in the pickup. There is something about uniting against, about scapegoating, that works. It keeps working (at some dried-up, shriveled-up little level) for me with my husband, my best friends, my colleagues, this church. We can scapegoat like crazy. But from the death and resurrection of Jesus, I do catch a glimpse of hope beyond that, how the unity we achieve through the old story is puny and half alive and lacking imagination and vitality in comparison with the communion possible in the love of God. The story of Jesus also reveals to me that God is not giving up on the transformation. I believe and hope that in spite of all our scapegoating deathishness, the gospel, this utterly life-giving, different story, frees us for communion based not on scapegoating, but on the transforming, forgiving love of God. I think you can see traces of it all around.

Debbie Blue has done an excellent job of rooting this proclamation of the atonement, not in stories or images from another era, but in stories from everyday life that her listeners can relate to. Like the biblical writers, however, she has not just connected with her audience; she has also utilized this presentation of the atonement to offer a strong challenge to normal patterns of living. Through presenting both the absorbing and transforming nature of the cross, she offers us a model of weaving together not just what the cross saves us from, but also what it saves us for. As she describes it, Christ's cross not only saves us from a tragically mistaken story, but also brings us forgiveness and enables us to live according to a new paradigm.

As mentioned in the introduction, Blue has utilized some of René Girard's thinking to illuminate this biblical text and the saving significance of the cross and resurrection. For those who are not familiar with Girard's work, and at the risk of oversimplifying his extensive work, I will briefly summarize some of his insights that lie behind Blue's sermon.[2]

Girard portrays Jesus as subverting the sacrificial system and offering a fundamentally different paradigm. People used spontaneous killing and scapegoating as a violent means to achieve something for themselves. Girard maintains that the sacrificial systems developed as a ritual reenactment of this victimization. Jesus undermines this victim mechanism both by offering and modeling grace and by championing victims. His commitment to nonviolence reveals the element of violence in institutions, including the temple and sacrifices. But Jesus also stands in the way of people's desires and expectations, everyone's: Romans, Pilate, Pharisees, and in the end even the disciples turn against him.

So all turn against Jesus in the classic and habitual human effort to resolve conflict by killing a common victim. But better than any other victim, Jesus reveals the true nature of this violent mechanism because he is the most arbitrary victim, the least violent. Jesus reveals how illegitimate the whole process is. He does not respond with violence but accepts being made a sacrifice; he offers forgiveness, again revealing the true nature of what is going on. The resurrection, however, is the key because it separates Jesus from all the other millions of innocent victims who have been tortured, expelled, and killed. This is something new; a victim comes back from the grave, not seeking vengeance, but offering forgiveness.

Scapegoating and sacrifice of victims brings temporary peace and reconciliation in a group only if it is hidden. If it is transparent, if we know we are killing X person (or group of people) as a way of bringing us together and resolving our conflicts, then it does not work. In regard to this dynamic, Jesus also subverts the mechanism. He illuminates, and thus frees us; he offers a different model.

Atonement as Drama in a Sunday School Class

Dan Whitmarsh

During the course of a junior high Sunday school class at Cornerstone Covenant Church in Turlock, California, the discussion turned to Mel Gibson's *Passion of the Christ*. Some of the students had seen it in the previous week, and they had several questions and issues they needed to have clarified. Eventually the discussion turned to the deeper meanings of it all, especially to the question "Why did Jesus do that?" As they talked, Dan Whitmarsh, who was teaching the class, thought about how he could formulate a response that this group of young people would be able to grasp. As typical middle-class boys and girls who had grown up in church and heard the classic "Jesus died to save us from our sins" line all their lives, they needed a fresh response that would push them to think deeper about the subject. What follows is his description of what he did that Sunday morning.

In response to my junior-highers' questions about Jesus's death on the cross, it occurred to me that perhaps acting it out might make it more understandable. The following is essentially what took place over the rest of the class period. The students acted and moved as I instructed them.

I chose two students, Eric and Becca, and had them stand and face each other. I said to the class, "Now, here is the nature of humanity. For one reason or another, intentional or not, Eric steps on Becca's toes. She is hurt and offended and feels that she must pay Eric back for his action, so she stomps on Eric's foot. Eric can hardly believe that Becca would hurt him like that, and to show his strength he kicks Becca in the shin. Becca, feeling unjustly attacked, knees Eric in the groin. Eric, after taking a moment or two to recover, is really angry, and he shoves Becca to the ground." As we moved through the escalating violence, Eric and Becca had fun pretending to hurt each other.

I went on with the story. "Now, see how this works? It happens all the time between individuals, between families, and between nations. Whatever the reasons for conflict are, it regularly builds up to the place where violence is done and people are hurt or killed. This is what we do to each other, and in a sense it's what we've done to God.

"If I were to ask you why Jesus died, you would probably say something like 'To take our place.' Then if I asked why he had to take our place, you'd probably say something like 'We sinned and so we had to die.' There is truth in both those statements, but they don't really approach the total meaning of what happened when we sinned, and when Jesus died in our place.

"First, you have to think about what actually happens when we sin. We tend to think of sin as breaking a rule in a book someplace. In reality, sin is more like when we hurt somebody else, when we do violence to another person. Eric isn't guilty of a sin because he broke a rule that said 'Don't kick people.' He's guilty of sin because he purposely hurt Becca. And this is true for Becca as well: she sinned not by breaking a rule against stomping on feet, but because she purposely hurt Eric.

"The same is true of our relationship with God. We aren't guilty in front of God because we broke some rule that God invented. We are guilty before God because we hurt him by deliberately choosing to do our own thing, to reject him, to live life without him. Adam and Eve's great sin wasn't in breaking the rule that said, 'Don't eat the fruit.' Their sin was in deciding, 'Hey—we can do whatever we want, regardless of what God said.' We also hurt God every time we hurt somebody else. If you were to hurt my daughter, I would be deeply distraught, because I love her. So, looking at Eric and Becca, you can tell how they've hurt each other, but you can also understand how they've hurt God, because he loves them and hates to see them damaging each other.

"Since we're back with Eric and Becca, let's look at where we stand. At this point in our little drama, they have done violence to God and to each other, and there really is no way out. Becca has been shoved to the ground, God has been cast aside, and everything is broken. Into this calamity stepped Jesus." At this point I picked another student, Chas, to be Jesus.

I'd done a lot of talking, so I thought it was time to get back to the action. Again, the three junior-highers acted out the story I was telling. "Let's say Becca picks herself back up. She and Eric face off for one final showdown. They pull their fists back in preparation for the fatal blow. Their arms move to deliver the punch, but just as they are about to hit each other, Chas jumps in the middle to protect them from each other and receives the blows instead. He falls to the ground, dead. Because he loves Eric and Becca, he has taken the blows intended for them, and he has paid the ultimate price.

"Yet look what happens. Chas gets back up. Eric and Becca did the worst they could to him: they killed him. How would you expect him to respond? By blowing them away, right? By pulling out the big guns and wiping them out? Instead, he comes back to Eric and Becca and embraces them. He loves them. He forgives them. Rather than fighting back, he comes back in peace. This offers hope to both Eric and Becca. Not only are they forgiven for killing Chas; they now also realize that they can stop fighting each other. Since Jesus has forgiven them, they can forgive each other. Since Chas embraced them in love, they can embrace each other. This cycle of revenge and violence can be put to an end.

"Do you see how this works? Jesus went to the cross as the result of the world of violence and rejection we have made. But Jesus came back in love, even after all the pain he endured. In the same way, we are stuck in this same broken world, but Jesus offers to free us from it. He endured the worst violence you can imagine, as many of you saw in the movie, and he went through that so you wouldn't have to. He went through all that and forgave those who did it to him. As I already pointed out, we reject God regularly in our choices, and he still forgives us. Our relationship with God, which has been broken, can be restored as we accept the forgiveness Jesus offers. Eric and Becca could keep on fighting, but they can also choose to accept the offer of peace given by Chas, and so live in a right relationship with each other and with God."

At that point I thanked the students and had them sit down, and the lesson ended.

This presentation focuses on themes that previous and future chapters in this book explore in more detail. I include it in this book, however, because of the concrete simplicity of the enacted drama. I appreciate the way it helped the youth sense the reality of sin and how Jesus entered into that reality to stop it, not just to enable some rearranging of heavenly legal ledgers. There is a powerful sense of God acting through the cross and resurrection to restore relationships. Dan Whitmarsh develops the drama in a way that portrays not just how Jesus stopped a cycle of sin and violence, but also how God responded in forgiveness—concrete forgiveness for concrete sins and wounds.

The Forgiveness of Sins
Hosea 11:1–9; Matthew 18:23–35

ROWAN WILLIAMS

Before he was the Archbishop of Canterbury, Rowan Williams preached this sermon in an Anglican worship service in Great Britain.[1] Here he takes an approach different from most others in this book. Rather than developing an image or metaphor to help communicate the saving significance of the cross, he explores a concept at the heart of the atonement—forgiveness. He uses human experiences and understandings of forgiveness as a means to illuminate the atonement and proclaim the profound forgiveness and possibility of new life available because of the cross of Christ.

Belief in forgiveness is just as much a matter of *faith* as anything else in the creed. It is no more obvious and demonstrable than the existence of God or the divinity of Jesus Christ. This is perfectly clear if we think a little about the meaning of forgiveness and the realities of human existence and relationship. I am what I am because of what I have been and done, good and bad. My self is woven out of a great web of complicated motivation, reflections, intentions, and actions, some of which have turned out to be creative, while others have been destructive for myself and for other people. And mature persons need to be able to see and accept all this, to take responsibility for some things and to accept the inevitability of others—to *own* the whole of ourselves, to acknowledge realities both past and present, to destroy all the crippling illusions about ourselves that lock us up in selfish fantasies about our power or independence. I depend on the past, and it is part of me; to deny it is to deny myself. I *am* my history.

People will often talk about forgiveness in a way that suggests this is not true. "Forgive and *forget*," we say; we'll say no more about it. We look at forgiveness as if it were the same as acquittal—leaving the court without a stain on our character, as if it simply obliterated the past. If that is how we think of forgiveness, it really *does* become incredible—an arbitrary fiat which unties all the knots we are bound in by simply pretending certain things haven't happened. It is rather like the attitude of those who seem to think that the resurrection cancels out the crucifixion. But we *know* this is not true: if we have been badly hurt by someone, then whatever happens the scars and memories will still be there, even if we "forgive" them. And if we have hurt someone, the same is true: we may be "forgiven," but we can see the effects of what we have done, perhaps for years after. If forgiveness is forgetting, then it isn't only incredible: it is a mockery of the depth and seriousness of the suffering that human beings inflict on each other. The monument at Auschwitz to the Jews killed there has the inscription, "O earth, cover not their blood." There are things that should never, never be forgotten—Auschwitz is one of them—and if forgiveness means forgetting, then forgiveness is a trivial and profoundly offensive idea, as that monument indeed suggests.

Well, though, isn't forgiveness still a possible idea even if we agree that the past can't be changed? Can't we say that forgiveness is an agreement not to forget, but at least to suspend judgment on the past? In other words, I deserve your anger, I deserve punishment, but you kindly excuse me what I owe you. This approach has a good deal of support in the New Testament; it is the basis of a lot of Christian thinking on the subject. I am a sinner, but God graciously treats me as if I weren't. This is important, and it is an advance on the "forgive and forget" idea. But is it enough on its own? Surely not. This is a forgiveness that changes nothing—something that sounds almost cynical if we're not careful. A forgiveness that says only, "I know exactly what you are and what you have done, but I'll say no more about it," can be, in fact, a terrible, negative judgment. I don't take you seriously enough to do anything: do what you like, I won't make any difficulties.

That's a travesty, of course, but it is something to beware of. No, we need something more positive to say about forgiveness. We need to recognize both the reality of the past and the hope of a future forgiveness. Because real forgiveness is something that changes things and so gives hope. The occasions when we feel genuinely forgiven are the moments when we feel, not that someone doesn't care what we do, but that someone *does* care what we do because he or she loves us and that love is strong enough to cope with and survive the hurt we have done. Forgiveness of that sort is creative because it reveals new dimensions to a relationship, new depths, new possibilities. We can find a love richer and more challenging than before. If someone says to me, "Yes, you have hurt me, but that doesn't mean it's all over. I forgive you. I still love you," then that is a moment of enormous liberation. It recognizes the reality of the past, the irreversibility of things, the seriousness of damage done, but then it is all the more joyful and hopeful because of that. Because this kind of love doesn't have illusions, it is also all the more mature and serious. It can look at and fully *feel* my weaknesses, and still say, "I love you."

But what does this say about the unhealed human injuries, about the death and catastrophe that can find no human resolution? Who is to forgive the camp commandant at Auschwitz, the murderer of a child, the tyrant waging genocidal wars? Only the victim has the "right" to forgive: I can't forgive on someone else's behalf. I can't intrude into that dreadful intimate relation between the one who hurts and the one who is hurt. So it seems as if there can be no forgiveness if the victim doesn't forgive—and the dead, you might say, don't forgive. We might find a reason for *pardoning* the murderer, but that is not the same thing. Are there, then, wounds never to be healed, personally as well as globally?

After all, our love is *not* very strong. It is hardly surprising if we come to a point where we say, "I can't take that. That is the end of love." Is forgiveness to depend on this, on our hopeless, inept struggles to love?

The reply of the gospel is "no." Christian faith here pushes right against the limits of the credible once again in saying that *God* forgives and has the *right* to forgive. God is the ultimate victim of all human cruelty, says the gospel: God bleeds for every human wound. Inasmuch as we do good or ill to any human person, it is done to God. Forgiveness is not only a matter to be settled among ourselves—or left unsettled because of our inadequacies. It is God's affair too. And the good news of Christianity is that, since God suffers human pain, since God is the victim of human injury, then there is beyond all our sin a love that is inexhaustible. God's love for this creation never comes to a point where it can take no more. In the old Prayer Book epistle for today, we hear Paul reminding us that *agapē*, God's love, never comes to an end. So God can always survive the hurt we do him; whenever we turn to him in sorrow and longing, after we have done some injury, this love is still there, waiting for us, a home whose door is always open. *Whatever* we do can never shut that door to his merciful acceptance. The only thing that can keep us out is the refusal to ask for and trust in that mercy.

And the gospel proclaims all this in virtue of the cross of Jesus. Without that, we cannot begin to understand the forgiveness of sins. Jesus crucified is God crucified, so we believe. Jesus is the total and final embodiment in history of God's loving mercy; and so this cross is a unique, terrible, extreme act of violence—a summary of all sin. It represents the human rejection of love. And not even *that* can destroy God: with the wounds of the cross still disfiguring his body, he returns out of hell to his disciples and wishes them peace. Because Jesus as preacher and teacher had proclaimed and enacted God's identification with the world of human beings, Jesus the condemned criminal speaks of God's presence in the extremity of suffering, in abandonment and death—God as victim. And thus he proclaims God as the one who, above all others, has the right to forgive. "In all their affliction he was afflicted." The prophet in the Old Testament saw a little of that, but here in Jesus it is spelled out in the detail of a human life and death. There is our hope—the infinite *resource* of God's love, the relationship with his creatures that no sin can finally unmake. He cares what we do because he suffers what we do. He is forever wounded, but forever loving. The possibilities of our relationship with him are indeed "new every morning."

So our sins become not stopping points, but starting points. They can be the occasions of constantly fresh, constantly *wider* visions of the grace of God. It's often been said, boldly, that the saints in heaven rejoice over their sins, because through them they have been brought to greater and greater understanding of the endless endurance of God's love, to the knowledge that beyond every failure God's creative mercy still waits. We have a future because of this grace.

A matter of *faith*: yes, indeed, not of clear knowledge or vision. To see God in Christ crucified is a matter of faith; to believe in the unyielding and inexhaustible love of God is a matter of faith; and to believe there is a future for us despite the reality of our sins is a matter of faith. Still more difficult to imagine is how God can forgive in the name of those most desperately and terribly hurt. How can God forgive the tyrant and the murderer? We can't talk too glibly about reconciliation and resolution here. It is hard to see how some people might ever let themselves be forgiven, even if forgiveness is offered. But it's not our business to work that out. All we can be sure of is that whatever the deficiency and the drying-up of human capacity to love, the killing of love by pain, there is still, at the heart of everything, a love that cannot be killed by pain. That is a warning against regarding or treating *any* human being as unforgivable; that is the positive side of this problem, this brick wall for the imagination. We don't know how some situations can issue in forgiveness, and we have to bear their dreadfulness without pious evasion, but it would be worse to deny the possibility of grace, however unthinkable. That possibility is our only hope, and it is the only clue to what "grace" can mean in our relations with each other—the refusal to set the limits to our love.

As Jesus' parable forcibly reminds us, the man who forgets how much and in what way he has been loved and forgiven, how much hurt he has inflicted on the eternal heart of God, and who clings to his "rights" and nurses his unforgiven injuries—that man is in mortal danger. He has understood nothing and sees forgiveness as a thing canceling the past. And of course he duly finds out that the past is not canceled. But we who profess belief in the forgiveness of sins must see forgiveness as something creative of the future, the future of our own love. It is never a possession; it is not something finished; it is a gift and a hope, and also a call.

The gift is itself a task. We can pray in gratitude to God for being forgiven, but we must pray too for help to live with forgiveness, and to *live* it in our own future.

Rowan Williams models for us an approach to contextualizing the message of atonement through leading his audience to reflect on their experiences of forgiving and being forgiven. Instead of starting with a concept or theory that may feel abstract or unintelligible and then working to connect it to life, he does the opposite. He leads the listeners to develop a concept of forgiveness from their experiences in life.

Although I would not endorse a theological approach that lets human experiences and reasoning serve as the foundation and guide for theological thinking,[2] at times (as here) human experience can function well as a means of communicating a theology rooted in God's self-revelation. For instance, Williams uses experience not to end up with a watered-down concept of forgiveness. Instead, through logic and reflection on real-life experience he leads the listener to sense the cost of forgiveness and also the impossibility of forgiveness being offered in some cases. In the process he helps the listener recognize that some of the things commonly said about forgiveness, in everyday life and sometimes in theological statements, do not match reality. We cannot forgive and forget. Simply suspending judgment can be a way of not taking seriously the hurt caused and communicating a sense of "Do what you like; I will not hold it against you."

In contrast, he helps us feel the richness of a forgiveness that acknowledges the hurt, that does not deny its pain and consequences, but states: "I forgive you. I still love you." He also, however, points out the impossibility of many receiving this forgiveness. There is no human way. It is a beautiful point of transition in the sermon. Is there then no way? The reply of the gospel is "no." At this point Williams turns our attention to the cross—the extreme act of violence and summary of all sin—to help the listeners comprehend both that the forgiveness God offers is true, deep, and rich, and that God can offer it to all.

Williams's proclamation on forgiveness has a different feel than many other presentations on the cross and forgiveness, not simply because of how he explores the theme of forgiveness in "real life," but also because of where he situates God. Rather than placing God in a legal system and saying that God is unable to forgive without first demanding punishment, Williams portrays God as the one most able to forgive, and entitled to do so, because of the pain and hurt God suffered at the cross. As in penal satisfaction, here the cross allows God to offer forgiveness to all, but for quite different reasons—reasons much more consonant with the theological guidelines derived from the New Testament writers (see chap. 1).

In an additional way Williams's sermon matches those theological guidelines for proclaiming the atonement: he not only communicates in a way that connects with his audience; he also challenges them. By referring back to the Gospel text they have heard, he not only proclaims forgiveness through the cross, but also calls them to be forgiving people.

Atonement

A Beach Parable for Youth

Mark D. Baker

Raymund Schwager's *Jesus in the Drama of Salvation: Toward a Biblical Doctrine of Redemption*[1] engaged me and provided new insights into the atonement. At one point in the middle of the book, however, I asked myself: "Sure, these are great insights, but could you explain this to your junior high Sunday school class?" What follows is a product of that question.[2]

A central purpose of this book is to provide examples of alternative images of the atonement. Theological discourse and discussion about the atonement is of vital importance. Unless, however, there is proclamation with images and stories that communicate nonpenal understandings of the atonement the majority of Christians will continue to be shaped only by images of penal substitution that assume a divine need to punish must be satisfied. I also recognize, however, that because many understand penal satisfaction to be *the* explanation of the atonement, they may tend to try to work alternative images into the paradigm of penal satisfaction rather than hear them as coming from a fundamentally different understanding of God's relationship with humanity. Therefore, I see the need not just to present alternative images of atonement, but also to relate those images to an alternative paradigm or foundational narrative.

Thus, in this parable, which combines my own thinking with insights from Schwager, I seek to root an image of atonement in a broader story that presents a fundamentally different concept of God the Father in relation to humanity and the cross, but also seeks to make a direct relationship between Jesus's life and the atoning work of the cross. I told this parable to the junior high class that I taught at College Community Church (Mennonite Brethren), Fresno, California. Following the parable I have included the discussion questions I used after I told the parable.

On the central California coast was a town that had no public beach. The twists and turns of the rocky coastline hid a number of sandy coves, but private estates completely surrounded all of them, and they had no public access.

A few years ago, an older man who owned one of these estates began feeling sorry for the local young people, who had to travel to the next town along the coast to swim, surf, or play on a beach. He decided to invite them to enjoy his beach. At all the local schools the man put up posters announcing that he was opening up his beach and telling the youth that they would find a clearly marked access path near his driveway on 342 Ocean Drive.

The man did not, however, simply open up the path. He thought carefully about helping the youths have as good a time as possible on the beach. He gathered up some old boogie boards, surfboards, and wetsuits from his garage, and even bought some used ones from a surf shop in a nearby town. The man could remember how frustrated he had been as a teenager when he could only stay in the cold water a little while because he didn't have a wetsuit like many others did. He had a local carpenter build a shed for storing the equipment and even put a few volleyballs and nets in it as well.

The owner welcomed all of the town's youth to use the beach and stated this plainly on the sign at the top, where the path led to the beach. Although the welcome was unrestricted, he did limit some activities. He wanted to enhance everyone's beach

experience and knew that too many people on a side in volleyball, or too many surfers trying to catch one wave, made it worse
for everyone. So he posted a sign on the beach that designated
one side of the beach for boogie boarding and swimming and
the other side for surfing. The sign stated that no more than
ten people at a time should surf (and if more wanted to surf,
they should work out a rotation system that would let all have
a chance). It also stated that no more than nine players should
be on each side in volleyball. The sign encouraged everyone to
remember to wear sunscreen. Finally, the sign invited the youth
to drop by and visit the owner as they left the beach. Many began
using the beach, and some did stop by, sit with him on his deck,
have a Coke, and talk for a while.

Although the man was too old to do much more than take
morning and evening walks on the shore, he loved sitting out
on the deck and watching others have fun on his beach. As the
months and seasons passed, however, he became confused and
concerned. Young people rarely stopped by to visit, and he observed that although most of those who did come to the beach
would stay for hours, others would leave soon after arriving. It
also seemed that fewer youth were showing up as time went by.
So the owner invited his grandson David, a teenager who lived
in a different state, to come and spend some time in the town
so that he could invite other youth to come to the beach and
encourage them to swim, surf, and play volleyball.

David spent his first day not at the beach, but around the
town, inviting the youth he encountered to come and hang out
at the beach. Their responses confused him. Some mumbled,
"Maybe," while others shuffled their feet, turned their eyes away,
and said something like, "Nah, I'm not into going to the beach
anymore." Most surprising was when someone bluntly said, "No
way: too many rules at that beach." David remarked in disbelief,
"What do you mean? There are only a few guidelines on the
sign." The teenager explained, "Well, it's not your grandfather's
sign that's the problem; it's what the beach clique say the sign
means, and the rules they have added. I mean, it used to be
that, because of the rule about only nine people being on a side
at a time, whenever more than eighteen people wanted to play
volleyball, we would set up another net. But now they say that
only the best eighteen people can play. Period."

Someone else added, "Yeah, and instead of taking turns surfing, they say that only people with new wetsuits can surf. That's how they make sure they can go surfing as much as they want." A younger girl jumped in: "Whenever we use the old wetsuits your grandfather put in the shed, they make fun of us and tell us not to come back unless we get nicer ones. They say, 'We don't want to be seen on the same beach as people in those ugly suits!'" Another boy spoke bitterly: "Sometimes they're mean like that, but other times they act real stuck-up and say things like 'The sign says to wear sunscreen, and you don't have shades on. You better go home or you might hurt your eyes.' But if you do wear shades that they don't think are cool, they make fun of you and say they don't want you around if you're going to look so stupid."

Finally an older Hispanic teenager added, "They even have a rule that only people who speak good English can be there. When I pointed to the sign, which says everyone is welcome, they said, 'But the sign is in English, and the owner speaks English; what the sign really means is that all youth who speak English good can use the beach.'"

David had heard enough. Clearly, one group of young people at the beach were making up rules to exclude those not in their group and insulting and embarrassing everybody else. "Who are these people," he asked, "this group that's making all the rules?" The teenagers around him told him to go to the beach and see for himself.

The next day David went to the beach to spend time with the people there. At first he thought the kids he had talked with the day before had been exaggerating. Although the young people on the beach were not overly friendly, they didn't seem so mean. In fact, when he told them he was the owner's grandson, they said quite nice things about his grandfather and told David how much they appreciated his grandfather letting them use the beach.

David enjoyed surfing with a few others and then joined a small group that was playing volleyball. Everything was going fine until a teenage boy, about his age, came over and asked if he could join the game. A girl sneered and said, "You know you aren't good enough. There are a lot more than eighteen people better than you, and only nine can play on a side."

The boy pointed at David; "How come you're letting *him* play? He's not part of your group." A boy from the other side of the net said, "But he's a good player like us, and even if you *were* better, I wouldn't want to be seen on the same volleyball court as you with such stupid shades. And where'd you get that swimsuit—from the nerd rack at Wal-Mart?" Suddenly David wondered how these people would have treated him if he wasn't a good player, or if he hadn't been wearing the new wetsuit his grandfather had given him for Christmas. He no longer doubted the complaints he had heard the day before.

That evening David told his grandfather all about what he had heard in town and what had happened at the beach. It saddened David to see his grandfather's pained expression as he listened to the report. David told his grandfather that when he had talked to the boy who had been put down and denied the chance to play volleyball, the boy had angrily said, "Tell your grandfather that he should teach those kids a lesson by kicking them off the beach as they've done to so many of us."

David's grandfather sighed. "I understand why some of the youth in town would love the feeling of revenge if I banned the clique from the beach. But kicking them off the beach would destroy the spirit of the beach. Actually, I guess we could say it would leave things the way they are right now, only with a different group excluded. No, David, we don't need to punish this group. If they don't change, sooner or later they'll find themselves hurt by the same rules and pressures to be cool that they are using against others right now. They will find themselves suffering humiliation and exclusion, just as they put down and exclude others." David interrupted: "How would that happen unless you go down and kick them off the beach yourself?"

His grandfather responded, "Maybe if you think of it the opposite way, it will help. If everyone on the beach accepted others and included them in their games, no one would have to worry about being disrespected or not fitting in. But this clique has drawn lines between insiders and outsiders, between good volleyball players and bad volleyball players, those who are cool and those who are not. Once those lines are drawn, even those who drew them have to make sure they stay on the right side of the lines. Even *now* some of them are suffering because of their own rules. Tonight a few are probably worrying that if more volleyball players as good as you show up, they'll be kicked out of the game. Others know that if they don't have enough money to get new wetsuits, sunglasses, and bathing suits every year, they might be ridiculed. And all of them have to wonder if people like them for who they really are, or only for their clothes and abilities. So we don't need to add to their punishment. If they stick to their rules, sooner or later those rules will kick them off the beach."

His grandfather paused for a moment and then said, "What we should do is warn them and try to show them a different way of living. I want you to go back to town tomorrow and invite the youth who have been excluded to come back to the beach with you. The popular kids won't include them, but you can set up your own volleyball net, and swim and surf with the ones who have been excluded. Now, there will likely be a confrontation. But it is important that in both your words and deeds you live out the fundamental rule of the beach: it is open for everyone to use and share, and that even includes the clique who wants to keep it for themselves. Don't try to take their surfboards away or anything like that. Instead, warn them about what I've just said."

When David showed up the next day with some people, all of whom had been insulted and shunned by the in-group for one reason or another, he noticed that the beach clique looked at him differently than they had the day before. When he set up a volleyball net and started playing with the people he had invited, the clique started insulting not just David's new friends, but also David himself.

Every day that week David brought some of the excluded youth with him to the beach and to visit with his grandfather. Although he focused on helping them feel as welcome as possible, not on upsetting the clique, inevitably every day there was a conflict—either because the clique didn't want to let the others go surfing, or just because their insults and threats were so strong that people would leave. Each time this happened, David would say firmly that the beach was for everyone, and then he would warn the clique that they would be much better off if they stopped shunning and insulting others. Stopping such action was the only way to avoid eventually being excluded and insulted themselves.

The popular kids became more and more upset with David because with him on the beach, their rules, threats, and scornful statements did not have the power they used to have. They wanted to chase him off the beach, but they feared that if they insulted him too directly, all the people he had been bringing might get upset and chase *them* off the beach.

The people in the clique came up with a plan. Over a couple of days they began including in their games and group some of those they had previously excluded. Then they did a lot of gossiping about David, about how he was ruining the beach for everyone.

One afternoon the clique started an argument with David over having two volleyball courts set up. They began yelling, "David must go! David must go!" They pointed, yelled, kicked sand, and threw the volleyball at him. Gradually those who had been playing on the other court with David melted away. Some of them even started yelling at David as well. One member of the clique picked up a rock and threw it at David's feet, yelling, "Get out of here, and don't come back!" Someone else threw a bottle that hit him. More rocks and bottles started flying, and one hit David on the side of the head and knocked him out. Most youths hurriedly left the beach; others swaggered away, sneering, "Bet he won't be causing trouble on the beach anymore."

After the clique and almost everyone else had left, a few of the young people cautiously walked over, kneeled down beside David, and then carried him up the path to his grandfather's house. He had recovered consciousness by the time they got to the door, but he was moaning and unable to stand without support. His grandfather opened the door, gasped, and cried out, "What happened?" But before they had a chance to answer, he was already telling them to put David in the car. As he rushed David to the hospital, one of the youths recounted what had happened. In the emergency room the grandfather sat beside David's bed, with tears streaming down his face. David needed stitches, many bandages, and a cast for a broken arm; he had to stay in the hospital for a few days.

While in the hospital David and his grandfather talked a lot about what had happened and how they should respond. His grandfather wrote a short letter to the youth of the town, which he later posted on the signs on the beach and at the start of the path leading to it:

> To those who hurt my grandson,
> You have made a tragic mistake and have done a horrible thing. You have insulted, hurt, and kicked off the beach the one person who had the most right to be there, someone from my family and hence an owner of the beach. As I desired, he sought to help everyone feel welcome and have a good time. Just as he already told you, your rules and insults did indeed lead to pain and exclusion. But David, not you, suffered that pain; and David, rather than you, was excluded. It can end here. There does not have to be any more exclusion. Anyone in town would agree that you deserve to be arrested and permanently kicked off the beach. But that is not my desire. I forgive you, and David forgives you. We will not press charges. My hunch is that hidden under all your cockiness, posing, and disrespecting others is not the confidence you display, but insecurity and fear. Our forgiveness gives you an opportunity to start over. I invite you to trust that my desire for the beach to be a place of welcome and inclusion is better for you, and a better way to lessen your insecurities and fears, than doing things that include some youths but embarrass and exclude others. I want nothing more than for my beach to be a place where all feel welcomed and accepted, and that includes each of you.

David's injuries kept him from going down to the beach in the few days left before he had to return to his home. He did, however, limp downtown to seek out some of his friends. Since some of them had actually joined the group in chasing David off the beach, and the rest had not stood up for him, they expected David to either ignore them or angrily demand to know why they had turned on him or not helped him. But David surprised them.

David greeted them warmly and invited them to join him for a Frappuccino, his treat. As they sat around a table, he repeated what his grandfather had said in the note: what the clique, and those who had joined it, had done was a horrible thing. But David and his grandfather were forgiving them. All of them could be confident that his grandfather would always let them go to the beach; there was no reason to fear him. And they could seek his forgiveness if they committed other wrongs on the beach in the future.

Most of them apologized to David in one way or another. One girl who had fallen under the influence of the clique when its members started including her, and who had energetically joined them in throwing things at David, sadly asked for forgiveness. She said, "I got sucked into it. I was out of control; it was like there was this power urging me on." David agreed and said that power would have grown even stronger if he had responded in the same way, seeking revenge by insulting, accusing, and trying to exclude those who had shamed and hurt him.

David went on to explain that he hoped this whole experience would lead the clique to stop insulting and excluding others, but he guessed that many members of the clique would keep doing their cliquish thing. David invited his friends, however, to think of him having already suffered in their place the worst sort of insulting and excluding they could experience. He said, "It did not crush me for good. See, I am here again, being accepted by you and sharing drinks and friendship with you right now. You can try to learn to shrug off their insults as I am doing. You don't have to let that clique's insults and rules determine what you do or how you feel. Go back and enjoy the beach!"

From that day on, the beach was a different place. The ugly scene of chasing David off the beach, followed by the forgiving note from David's grandfather, seemed to shake up and transform some of the members of the clique, and they became more relaxed about what they wore to the beach or how good they were in volleyball. They also stopped making fun of others, and more frequently they spent time visiting with David's grandfather. As David predicted, however, some of them did not change. They continued to insult and laugh at others, but if they would have been honest enough to admit it, they were even more insecure than they had been before, in part because their words did not seem to have the same power that they used to have.

But other youths came and put on the old wetsuits from the storage shed or got out a volleyball net, and they seemed unaffected by the same insults that had kept them away before. Surprisingly, those without expensive shades or new swimsuits and some who spoke with an accent did not simply ignore the insults; from time to time they also actually invited those insulting them to join in a game, or catch a wave together.

Discussion Questions

1. What are some things you have seen or experienced that are similar to this parable?
2. How would the story have changed if David and his grandfather had sought revenge and pressed charges against the young people?
3. Parables are stories that use things familiar to us to help us understand things that are less familiar or harder to understand. In parables not every detail in the story exactly matches what it represents, but there are strong similarities. If we think of David as being Jesus and the grandfather as being God the Father, how does this story help us understand how Jesus's life led to his death on the cross? Why was he crucified?
4. Does relating the parable to Jesus's life, death, and resurrection give you any new ideas about the cross and resurrection and why they are so important to Christians? Please share some of those ideas with the group.
5. What was the difference between the grandfather's rules for the beach and the clique's rules?
6. How is the grandfather in the story similar and different from the way you imagine God?
7. How does Jesus's life, death, and resurrection invite us to live differently?
8. Think of recent times when you have felt excluded or humiliated by others. How can Jesus's life, death, and resurrection provide help in a time like that? (You could think about how what David went through helped the youths of the town to not be as affected by the insults and taunting.)
9. Think of recent times when you have felt guilty. How can Jesus's life, death, and resurrection provide help in a time like that?
10. This last question is for you to think about and write an answer. We will not share it with others. David and his grandfather demonstrated an attitude of welcome and acceptance and spoke words of forgiveness, encouragement, and challenge to the youth in the parable. What might God be saying to you today?

As stated in the introduction, through this parable I seek to situate the atonement in a broader narrative of God's gracious initiative and Jesus's life. I trust that the parable communicates various theological and biblical elements clearly enough that you could adapt it for use in your own context. I would, however, like to make more explicit the thinking behind two elements in the parable because of how they differ so significantly from common presentations of penal substitutionary atonement.

In the first chapter of this book, I stated that my critique is not with substitutionary atonement, but with a particular version of substitutionary atonement—penal substitution, which portrays God as punishing Jesus instead of punishing us humans. This parable presents an alternative view of Jesus: he stands in the place of humans and suffers the judgment that humans deserve. In this parable, however, God neither demands that punishment as a condition for offering forgiveness nor is God the author of the punishment. This aspect of the parable is based on the following interpretation of Jesus's life.

Those who killed Jesus acted out a tragedy we all are involved in. Jesus proclaimed a message of radical graciousness and acceptance, and then he lived out that message. Many, however, resisted and rejected the kingdom of God as lived and proclaimed by Jesus. In response, Jesus spoke words and parables of judgment. In doing so, however, he did not retract his message of unconditional love, of invitation to all to join him in table fellowship. He did not say, "You have not done what is necessary to achieve God's love and acceptance." Rather, out of loving concern he warned them of the consequences to themselves and others that would come from their rejecting God's graciousness and rooting themselves ever more firmly in a society of tit-for-tat reciprocity, in a religiosity of status seeking and drawing lines of exclusion, and fundamentally, in a paradigm that mistakenly imagined a God of conditional love. They would suffer, as well as cause others to suffer, the real punishments of that society and religiosity and live in fear of the "God" they believed in.[3]

In his unrelenting and gracious effort of love and inclusion, however, Jesus took on himself the fate that he had warned others about. Jesus had not sinned, but he bore the ultimate consequences of our sin, of our lack of trust in God. We can say that Jesus died for us by entering into our situation and shouldering the ultimate consequences of an alienation that was ours, not his. He suffered in our place to save us from suffering the ultimate consequence of our sin.

The parable seeks to root atonement, the cross, and resurrection in the concreteness of Jesus's life on earth rather than portraying the actuality of the atonement as being a transaction involving heavenly legal ledgers, rather than seeing the crucifiers of Jesus as unwittingly playing a role in something that had to happen to allow God to adjust our legal status in heaven. One of the ways the parable seeks to do this is by making forgiveness a central part of the actual drama and not just an action enabled by the drama of the cross.

At the cross humans acted out our unbelief and alienation. God experienced the worst that humans could do. Jesus suffered a humiliating and painful death, and God the Father suffered the loss of his son through that shameful means of execution. Yet on that cross Jesus prayed, "Father forgive them; for they do not know what they are doing" (Luke 23:34 NRSV). When Jesus forgave those who crucified him, he forgave them not just for the specific act of crucifixion, but also and more profoundly for the attitudes and behaviors that had led to the cross. He forgave them for their rejection of the gracious God revealed by Jesus and the rejection of the true humanity modeled by Jesus. God, however, provides more than a decree of forgiveness. Through the resurrection Jesus returned to the disciples as a concrete forgiving presence, intent not on scolding, shaming, or seeking revenge for their betrayal and desertion, but on reaching out in love and restoring relationships.

God had forgiven before, and Jesus had previously demonstrated a forgiving stance to his disciples and others; but the depth of the offense at the cross means that God's forgiveness of that offense also reaches down to the very depth of human sin: God has and will forgive the worst we can do. The powerful waves of that forgiveness extend to the twenty-first century, making forgiveness available to people for their acts of "crucifixion" as they reject God, hurt and step on others, and reject their true humanity. Through this forgiving action God removes a barrier that stands between humans and God.

Made New by One Man's Obedience

Romans 5:12–19

Richard B. Hays

In *Recovering the Scandal of the Cross*, we sought to listen to how the New Testament writers spoke of the saving significance of the cross before discussing various theories of atonement, and we sought to hear individual New Testament writers speaking for themselves rather than let one voice, Paul's, drown out the rest. More accurately, one could say that many have read select Pauline passages through the lens of a penal satisfaction theory and have let that voice drown out other voices—even other voices in Paul.

In this sermon, preached in a chapel service at the Duke Divinity School on February 17, 2005, Richard Hays helps us hear with clarity another Pauline voice speak about Jesus Christ's saving work. We begin with his translation of the text.

Therefore, just as Sin came into the world through one man, and Death through Sin, and thus Death spread throughout the human race, with the result that all sinned—

(For before the Law came, Sin was indeed in the world, but since there was no Law, sin was not counted up; nonetheless, Death reigned. Death reigned from Adam to Moses, even over those who did not sin in the likeness of the transgression of Adam [by violating a commandment].)

Now Adam is the *type* of the Coming One.

But the grace-gift is *not* like the false step. For if by the false step of the one man the many died, *how much more* has the grace of God overflowed by means of the grace of the one man Jesus Christ to the many.

And the gift is *not* like the effect of the one man's sin. For the judgment issuing from the sin of one led to condemnation; but the grace-gift following upon many false steps leads to vindication.

For if, by virtue of the one man's false step, Sin reigned through the one man, *how much more* will those who receive the superabundance of grace and of the gift of righteousness—how much more will they reign in life through the one man Jesus Christ.

So then, as through the false step of one man condemnation came to us all, so also through the righteous act of one man the rectifying of life came to us all.

For just as through the disobedience of one man the many were constituted as sinners, so also through the obedience of one man the many were constituted as righteous. (Rom. 5:12–19)

If the apostle Paul had turned this passage in to me as a short theological reflection paper, I would have told him, "Get thee to the writing tutor." Then I would have called up John Utz in the Center for Theological Writing and told him, "This guy Paul has some weighty ideas, but you really need to help him with this essay. First of all, he begins it with a sentence fragment. Then he goes off on a couple of digressions before he gets back to his main point. And he keeps repeating himself; it looks as though he was trying out different formulations on the word processor and then just turned in his rough draft without going back to edit it. The logical transitions are rather awkward. Finally, he could really use some illustrations to help us follow the point he's trying to make. I hope you can straighten him out so that he can pass my course on Greek Exegesis of Romans."

Joking aside, I suspect that the difficulty we have with this passage signals that it is *we*, not Paul, who need some remedial work. At the superficial level, we need remedial work because we have lost the patience and skill necessary to follow intricately woven theological arguments. We would prefer our theology articulated in prose aimed at a fifth-grade reading level. But the deeper truth is this: we need remedial work because we have followed our father Adam on the slippery path of false steps, and we have fallen. So we find ourselves under the sway of the powers of Sin and Death. And living under these illusion-spinning powers, we have lost sight of the true story that makes sense of our lives.

Where then shall we begin the remediation?

First, we have to recognize our true condition as people caught in the web of Sin and Death. We don't like to think about that. We like to believe that we have things under control, that down deep we are good, and that all the world's problems come from somewhere else—an "axis of evil" or some aberrant fringe group. We like to believe that given enough time and ingenuity, we will solve our problems and "build a better world." Do we fear violence? We can solve that problem: we just have to kill all the bad people. (I saw a bumper sticker the other day, though, that said, "We're making enemies faster than we can kill them.") Social and economic ills? We just need to elect the right candidates and appoint the right Supreme Court judges. Psychological problems? We just need to find the right prescription drugs to achieve equilibrium. Our universities and corporations are now engaged in fierce competition to perfect techniques of genetic engineering, so that we can redesign our own bodies and eliminate the flaws. O brave new world!

Even death is sometimes regarded as a problem medical science has not yet solved, . . . but give us time. Some of you may remember the gruesome fate of Ted Williams, the great Boston Red Sox slugger: after his death a couple of years ago, his son had his body frozen to preserve it (hung upside down in a tank of liquid nitrogen at 325 degrees below zero) in the hope that a future medical science would find a way to restore life. (I guess if the Red Sox can win the World Series, anything is possible!) All of this bears witness to our pathetic self-deceiving desire to hide from our own mortality, and our own sinfulness.

In the opening chapters of Romans, Paul relentlessly hammers on this theme. Like Adam and Eve, we have turned away from God into disobedience, and the end of our proud attempt to be "like God, knowing good and evil" (Gen. 3:5 NRSV) is that we fall into idolatry, confusion, and self-destructive violence—all the while imagining ourselves to be virtuous. So the story of Adam holds a mirror before us, a mirror in which we can begin to glimpse our nakedness and shame. Adam's story is our story. And once that story is set in motion, human history becomes a chain reaction of deception, hiding behind fig leaves, violence. The second chapter in the story of Adam is the account of Cain and Abel. If you want a clear image of what that chapter looks like, I urge you to see the film *Hotel Rwanda*.

The second step in our remediation is not to be unduly impressed by the grimness of our own situation. Not because it isn't terrible, but because the gospel offers the overwhelming good news that "Christ died for the ungodly" (Rom. 5:6 NRSV). Despite our blindness and violence, we have now received reconciliation through Jesus Christ. One of the striking features of Romans 5:12–19 is Paul's adamant insistence on the *asymmetry* between sin and grace. Listen: "But the grace-gift is *not* like the false step. For if by the false step of the one man the many died, *how much more* has the grace of God overflowed by means of the grace of the one man Jesus Christ to the many." That "how much more" (*pollō mallon*) is the hallmark of Paul's gospel. As Paul Achtemeier puts it, "Thus does grace triumph over evil, by burying evil in an avalanche of grace."[1]

That is why the analogy between Adam and Christ is *only* an analogy. Our solidarity with Adam in sin, confusion, and death is only a pale, negative, two-dimensional shadow of our much more real, three-dimensional solidarity with Jesus Christ. Curiously, our powers of perception are so impaired that we find it easier to grasp our solidarity with the old death-bound humanity in Adam than to grasp our participation in the new life-giving humanity into which Christ's death and resurrection have placed us. That is why Paul reminds us of Adam: to give us a clue, a mental handhold from which we can begin to grope toward imagining how our destiny can be determined by the action of a single great figure who comes before us and shapes the reality in which we live. But the Adam-Christ analogy should never mislead us into thinking that Jesus Christ merely undoes the effects of Adam's transgression and puts us back at square one with a blank slate. Instead, Jesus has swept us into a new creation in which our identity is now positively redefined by his faithfulness rather than by our own disloyalty to God.

This way of speaking already points to a third crucial recognition. (And I carefully select the word *crucial*.) According to Romans 5, it is the *obedience* of Jesus Christ on which our salvation hangs. Adam broke the commandment, and death entered the world. Israel violated the Sinai covenant, came under the curse, and went away into exile. But the story of Jesus's temptation in the wilderness reveals that something new has happened in the world. Jesus reveals himself as the new Adam, who rejects the temptation to be like God and to seize power. Jesus is also the true Israel, who rightly honors the Torah by taking refuge in the words of Deuteronomy 6:13: "Worship the Lord your God, and serve only him" (Matt. 4:10 NRSV). And the wilderness temptation certainly is a dress rehearsal for the true climax of Israel's story. The climax is this: Jesus's obedience extends all the way to his death on a cross, still embodying his fervent prayer: "May your will be done" (cf. Matt. 6:10; 26:42). That is why Jesus's obedience quite literally initiates a new humanity, a new creation. Because of him and in him, the story can begin again.

Romans 5 offers one final point for reflection, as we undertake the remedial work of allowing Paul's gospel to transform our minds. *In what way* does the death of Jesus bring about our reconciliation with God? (Or, to use the language of the systematic tradition, what theory of atonement do we find in Romans 5?)

In the Protestant tradition, particularly in its evangelical forms, we are used to interpreting the atonement chiefly in terms of blood sacrifice and penal substitution: Jesus paid the penalty that rightly was ours. Jesus shed his blood as a victim in order to cleanse us from guilt and sin—and perhaps to appease the wrath of God. To be sure, Paul does occasionally use images of substitutionary atonement (e.g., Rom. 3:24–25; 5:9).[2] Yet such references are surprisingly rare. Paul almost never talks about "forgiveness of sins," because—and here is the key point—he has a more radical diagnosis of the human predicament and a more radical vision of new creation. We need far more than forgiveness or judicial acquittal. We need to be *changed*. We need to be set free from our bondage to decay and liberated to participate in the life of the world to come, a life that has already invaded our broken world. Strikingly, Romans 5:12–19 says nothing about blood sacrifice. The Adam-Christ typology offers a quite different picture of the way in which we are saved: we are saved because we participate in the new humanity that Jesus, the faithful and obedient one, inaugurated.

How shall we picture this? Consider an analogy. Sometimes a computer can become so infected by a virus that it is necessary to erase the memory on the hard disk and start over, reinstalling the software—including the operating system—and rebooting the machine. That is a distant analogy to what Paul is saying in Romans 5. It is as though the human race in Adam has become so infected by the virus of sin that malfunctions and "illegal operations" are paralyzing the system. Jesus, by virtue of his radical obedience to God, erases the infected program and installs a new virus-resistant operating system, enabling us to function rightly for the purpose for which God constructed us. Jesus thus is Humanity 2.0.

Nevertheless, we are not machines, and for that reason I worry about this analogy. Perhaps it is more like this: we are a dysfunctional family, caught in cycles of misunderstanding, infidelity, conflict, and abuse. Jesus arrives in the midst of our domestic troubles—as a mysterious, long-lost older brother—and transforms the family by living a new self-giving way. He thereby astonishingly changes the destructive dynamics and refocuses the family on the love of God. His faithfulness not only *models* a different pattern of life but also actually *creates* a new kind of family.

Once again, analogy falls short. I find myself wanting to say, like Paul, "But the grace-gift is not like the virus-riddled computer; how much more has the grace of God overflowed by means of the grace of the one man Jesus Christ." Or again, "But the grace-gift is not like the squabbling family; how much more has the grace of God overflowed by means of the grace of the one man Jesus Christ." This overflow of grace has actually *constituted* us a new people, a new creation. That is the reality toward which all our analogies grope. And so we have peace with God, through our Lord Jesus Christ.

Thanks be to God!

As a New Testament scholar, Richard Hays has spent years immersing himself in Paul's writings. In this sermon we benefit from that immersion. Even as Hays talks about Paul, the language he uses has a Pauline character. In one sense this is a simple straightforward sermon. Yet through reading this passage with the rest of the letter in mind, and through letting these verses speak, rather than muffling them with concepts and traditions brought from other places, Hays preaches a powerful message of our lostness, met by God's grace and transformational salvation. It is a salvation that is richer, fuller, broader, and more radical than understanding Christ's saving work only in terms of forgiveness of sins. That does not mean it is inappropriate to have a presentation of the atoning work of Christ that focuses on forgiveness; nevertheless, this sermon helps us realize what is missed if that is the only way we proclaim the saving significance of the cross.

Hays not only describes Paul's teaching with clarity; he also helps his listeners contextualize Paul's message through relating it to contemporary events and through the two analogies he offers at the end of the sermon. These analogies help us grasp the radical nature of Jesus Christ's new-creation work. Hays thus aids us in comprehending what God has done through Christ. Yet many of us live in individualistic societies with an atomistic understanding of reality; hence, we find it hard to understand how Jesus has done this. How is it that one person "not only models a different pattern of life but also actually creates a new kind of family"—creates a new humanity? Paul presents Jesus and Adam as individuals affecting the corporate whole. Paul's first-century readers would have found that concept easier to grasp than many of us do. In the next chapter, Steve Taylor looks for contemporary analogies that make the "how" of Christ's representative role more intelligible in his contemporary New Zealand context.

Participation and an Atomized World

A Reflection on Christ as Representative New Adam

STEVE TAYLOR

Most of the contributors to this book have immersed themselves in the biblical narrative, sought to understand its images of atonement, and then developed new images and metaphors to proclaim, as the biblical writers did, the scandalous reality of the cross and its saving potential. This approach recognizes that a metaphor having deep meaning in one context will not necessarily communicate in another. Aware of this reality, Steve Taylor does not simply use biblical language and images with the assumption that they will communicate to his audience in twenty-first-century New Zealand. For instance, in this sermon he preached at Opawa Baptist Church in Christchurch in May 2004, he recognizes that the notion of Jesus as the representative "new Adam" does not connect with people living in an individualistic society, with an atomized understanding of the world. Rather than discarding the biblical language and image, however, Taylor digs into the contemporary context and experience of New Zealanders and finds remnants of the corporate worldview that can help them understand salvation coming through our incorporation into Jesus Christ, our representative. Taylor uses contemporary images to breathe new life and meaning into biblical images.

A diamond is an object of love and beauty.[1] It is a gift given and received at precious, intimate times. To fully appreciate a diamond and all of its depth and intricacies, we need to turn it. We need to see all the faces and watch how different lights make the diamond dance in different ways.

The gospel of the life, death, and resurrection of Jesus is like a diamond. It is a gift of love, given and received at precious, intimate times. It has many faces, and to appreciate it fully, we need to see them all: Jesus as a victor, a sufferer, a martyr, a sacrifice, a redeemer, a reconciler, a justifier, an adopter, and a representative.[2]

So, leading up to communion throughout this year, I am going to be turning the diamond of the gospel. I do not want to be a pastor that shrinks the gospel. Nor do I want to offer you only one side of the diamond. I want communion to be for us a time of love, a precious, intimate time. I want communion to be about depth; we watch as different lights make all the faces of the diamond dance in new ways.

Today, I want to polish the diamond face of Jesus as our representative, as our new Adam.

In 2 Corinthians 5:14–15 we read: "We are ruled by Christ's love for us. We are certain that if one person died for everyone else, then all of us have died. And Christ did die for all of us. He died so we would no longer live for ourselves, but for the one who died and was raised to life for us" (CEV).

Jesus is our representative, one person who died for everyone, one person who was raised to life for all of us. The culture of Jesus's time had an integrated view of life and a strong faith in the power of representation. In this world, one person could represent all the people. And so the apostle Paul calls Jesus a new Adam. As Adam represents all of humanity, so Jesus as new Adam represents a new humanity. Thus Paul says, "Adam sinned, and that sin brought death into the world" (Rom. 5:12 CEV). And, "Jesus Christ alone brought God's gift of kindness to many people" (5:15 CEV).

As Adam represents humanity, so Jesus as new Adam represents a new humanity.

Let us unpack the two:

Adam sinned	Christ is sinless
Adam disobeyed	Christ obeyed
sin enters our world	grace enters our world
Adam dies	Christ dies to end fallen humanity
Adam stays dead	Christ resurrected, a new human
Adam ushers in era of enmity	Christ ushers in era of life
old creation	new creation
what we are	what we can become
Adam	new Adam

Such pairs tempt us to think of balance. Adam, the old representative, unites us in death; Jesus, the new representative, unites us in life. Yet balance ignores the God of the equation. For God, life engulfs death. The new representative overwhelms the old representative. Such is grace.

The representative face of the gospel diamond glitters against the velvet background of the chapters surrounding 2 Corinthians 5. We are faced with the beauty that is the shared participation in the new creation. Do you want to have life and to the full? You can, through the new human. You can, because Christ "died so we would no longer live for ourselves, but for the one who died and was raised to life for us" (2 Cor. 5:15 CEV).

Let me introduce one critical thought, one arms-folded question. The people of Jesus's day believed that one person could represent all of humanity. For instance, their worldview accepted that because of Adam, all of humanity was disobedient and sinful. The world of Jesus had kings and rulers. The king was the leader. When the king spoke or acted, he was the representative of the people. And so when the king acted in sin, all the people were sinful.

We see this idea of ruler as representative at work in J. R. R. Tolkien's *The Return of the King*, part 3 of *The Lord of the Rings*.

We catch a flashback to a representative, ancient world. The Steward of Gondor orders an attack on the invading orc army. It is a stupid attack. Everyone advises the Steward not to order the attack, even his own son. Yet they must obey the Steward. His son leads the attack and is nearly killed. This is the worldview of Jesus's era. One ruler speaks on behalf of all people. One person's actions affect all people.

Our world is not Jesus's world. Nor is it the world of *The Lord of the Rings*. We live in an individualized, Western world. When our ruler, our leader, our prime minister speaks or acts, I don't always agree, nor do you. As individualized Westerners, we all express our own opinions. In our world, one person does not speak or act for everyone.

Here now is the critical thought, the arms-folded question: How can Adam's actions and Jesus as representative include independent, free-acting me?

Yet think with me for a moment. Perhaps we do have our representatives. First, we do have representative New Zealanders. Look at our banknotes. On our five-dollar note is a portrait of Sir Edmund Hillary.[3] When we think of Hillary, we think of toughness, focus, humility, and giving, values that we believe represent the best of New Zealanders. Hillary sums up many qualities representative of being a New Zealander. His values represent values to which we aspire. Even today in New Zealand there are times when one person does represent all the people. So it is logical for us to see Jesus as on the banknote of Christianity, summing up all that represents being human. Jesus: loyal, healing, caring, deeply connected to God and people. Jesus is the representative of the truest human values.

Second, if your arms are still folded, we do have those treaty-signing ceremonies, a peace accord between two warring nations, or a trade deal between two countries. We see them on TV. People sign, shake hands, and two parties, two groups, two communities are now bound by that agreement. Two groups of people have agreed to work together, and representatives sign the legal agreement. A person signs on behalf of the community. And so it is logical to see Jesus as signing a peace accord on our behalf. Once there was enmity between us and God, us and others, us and God's earth. Yet Jesus signs for us, thus enacting a peace accord between us and God, us and others, us and God's earth. Jesus is representative of the community.

Third, if your arms are still folded, from the movie *Whale Rider*, we have another example of a representative figure.[4] The grandfather, Koro, is searching for a savior, someone to lead the village. Near the end of the movie is a scene with a pod of whales stranded on the beach. The villagers have tried all night to turn the whales around and head them out to sea. They have no success. They are tired and wet, dejected and defeated. As they trudge back up the beach, the young girl Paikea steps toward the whale. "If the whale lives, we live," she says in the book *The Whale Rider*. She greets the whale. She finds indentations and footholds and climbs onto the whale. She rides the whale out to sea. In doing so, she is willing to give up her life. The whales dive into the sea. Paikea prepares to die.

The village fears that she is drowned, and the people mourn. Yet three days later she is found. On her recovery bed, her grandfather promises to follow her, as a wise and honored teacher. *The Whale Rider* ends with grandfather and granddaughter hearing the whales singing. There is a new harmony between humans and their environment.

The movie *Whale Rider* ends with Paikea and Koro riding a canoe out to sea. The entire village is gathered. Estranged family members have returned. The previously alienated are welcome. Many visitors are present. There is the birth of a new community, a new inclusion, a fresh welcome to those previously distant. Through Paikea's act, a new sense of community and identity is born in her village. Through her act, the villagers discover a new sense of community between humans and the environment. And so Paikea has given her life for her people. By her actions, discernment, and act of sacrifice, there is a new future for this community. The act of one who died and was raised to life has become the vehicle, the representative, through which the people discover a new way of being human.

In a similar way, Jesus is our representative, our new Adam. He was willing to act as representative, as savior on our behalf. He was willing to die for the people. Three days later he was raised to life. In this act we are offered a place in a new community and invited to participate in harmony with our environment.

The estranged and alienated are welcome. Through Jesus as representative, we are enfolded into a new community.

So, we have asked the arms-folded question: How can Adam's sin and Jesus as representative include independent, free-acting me? And yet, we do have our representatives:

Representatives of human values: And so we are offered Jesus on the banknote of Christianity, summing up all that it means to be human: loyal, healing, caring, deeply connected to God and people.

Representatives of the community: And so we are offered Jesus, who has signed a treaty to bring peace between warring factions.

Representatives who enfold us into a new community: And so we are offered Jesus, who has acted on our behalf to enfold us into a new community in harmony with God's creation.

Jesus is our representative, one person who died for everyone, one person raised to life for all of us.

As we come to communion, I think of two applications: first, it is time to die. Jesus as representative invites us to die. In the Garden of Eden, Adam chose to do what he wanted, to live life his own way. German theologian Dietrich Bonhoeffer, who died for his faith, called Jesus "the man for others."[5] The new Adam lives for others. The old Adam lived self-absorbed for himself. It is time for us, like Paikea, to be prepared to die. It is time for us to say, "I want to stop living for myself." And so our Christian baptism becomes a physical and symbolic way of saying, "I will go down into the water; I will go down to die." Jesus as representative asks us to die to the old Adam.

Second, it is time to live. Jesus as representative invites us to live. As Paul says in Galatians 2:20: "It is no longer I who live, but it is Christ who lives in me. And the life I now live . . . I live by faith in the Son of God, who loved me and gave himself for me" (NRSV). When we die to the old Adam, we are able to live "in Christ." We are part of the new Adam. What does this actually look like? Well, for me it means to relax and just enjoy being in Christ. There is no end zone that I must try to reach. There is a whole "in Christ" field that I can run around on. Christ has done the hard yards. Christ as the new Adam, has lived all of life the way God intended. It is time for me to relax and enjoy that life.

Time to die, time to live—two applications as we come to communion.

In conclusion, together we have turned the diamond. We have let the light sparkle on one face, on Jesus as representative, as new Adam. This is the gospel. If we die to the old Adam, we can live with the new Adam.

———

As I stated in the first chapter, many have incorrectly interpreted *Recovering the Scandal of the Cross*'s critique of penal substitution as a critique of substitutionary atonement in general. These previous two chapters (9–10) offer examples of how one can proclaim a substitutionary atonement without it having a penal character. As Christopher Marshall states, "It is true . . . that Paul sees a *substitutionary dimension* to Christ's death. But is substitutionary not in the sense of one person replacing another, like substitutes on a football team, but in the sense of one person *representing* all others, who are thereby made present in the person and experience of their representative. Christ died not so much instead of sinners as on behalf of sinners, as their corporate representative."[6] Perhaps in using images and metaphors like those Hays and Taylor explore, we can begin to proclaim this aspect of Paul's writings in understandable and transformative ways today.

We do not, however, have to go all the way back to Paul to find robust and articulate use of the "Christ as representative" theme in writings about the atonement. Irenaeus's recapitulation theory of the atonement has strong affinities with this Pauline idea.[7] Therefore, Hays and Taylor not only stand on firm biblical ground as they develop this theme. They also are in line with fine theological work done by one of the church's early theologians.

The Cross
as Prophetic Action

Brian D. McLaren

Brian McLaren preached the following sermon in the summer of 2003 at Cedar Ridge Community Church in Spencerville, Maryland—a non-denominational church with an intentional sensitivity to unchurched and postmodern people. The sermon was part of a series the pastoral team preached on the Minor Prophets. McLaren offers the following reflection on the sermon: "As I developed a message on the ordeal of Hosea, I felt I gained new insight into an important—perhaps essential?—understanding of the cross of Jesus. This understanding takes the question of the cross's significance outside the parameters of penal substitution theory, and in fact outside the parameters of substitutionary atonement theory entirely. I present this not as the only or true way to see the meaning and purpose of the cross, but perhaps as an under-appreciated way, one window among many others into an expansive, deep, soaring mystery."

Jesus was more than a prophet, but he was also not less than a prophet. In the end, people couldn't squeeze him into any existing categories; but in the beginning of his ministry, it was within the category of a prophet that the people tried to understand him. Most important, Jesus described himself and his work by making comparisons to various prophets on more than one occasion. By better understanding the role and work of prophets, we can better understand Jesus—and his death and resurrection—in needed and corrective ways.

Saying this doesn't help much, because too many people have something worse than ignorance regarding the role and work of prophets. Too many people think that a prophet is by definition a fortune-teller, a future-forecaster, a prognosticator. Prognostication is a prophetic function, but a relatively minor one, and even that role is easily misunderstood.[1] The major prophetic role is broader: to bring the word of the Lord to bear on a specific situation, and to bring people to a point of decision on how they will respond. Prophets cannot compel obedience: they never bear the sword; they always come with vulnerability to being disbelieved, disregarded, rejected, persecuted, killed. But even though they cannot compel obedience, they do precipitate a decision one way or the other.

It's helpful to contrast the role of the prophet with the role of the priest. In ancient Israel the priests had official functions, and there was a standard protocol for becoming a priest. Prophets, however, arose ad hoc. They had no credentials except the message they carried. Before receiving and conveying a divine message, the prospective prophet could have been a priest (as Jeremiah was), but one could just as easily have been a shepherd (like Amos), a widow (like Anna in the New Testament), or something else.

Priestly work established and supported the regular ongoing religious life of the people; prophetic work interrupted that religious life when apathy, complacency, and self-obsessed personal piety set in. Priestly work was rule- and ritual-oriented, fastidious, and largely routine (handling sacrifices, cleaning, inspecting), with a quietly evocative, steady artistic dimension (such as the unchanging design of the tabernacle and temple, or the unchanging fragrance of the special anointing oil). In contrast, prophetic work was unpredictable, unprecedented, and unrepeated, bold and grand, artistic in a way that moved from gently evocative to stunningly provocative. Beyond their more daring and extreme poetic language, they often used the high drama of what we might call performance art—intrusive, scandalous, shocking at times—to make their messages both unavoidable and unforgettable. For example, at times their dramatic enactments, sometimes called "prophetic action," used nudity, excrement, and other shocking features. The blinder the people, the harder their hearts, the duller their ears—the louder and the more bizarre the prophetic message had to be to get their attention.[2]

One prophet, Hosea, delivered a message purely by prophetic action first, and later he explicated it with poetic words. Hosea lived in a slice of that tumultuous period between about 950 and 450 BC. It was after the Jewish people's greatest king, David; after his promising but ultimately disappointing son King Solomon; after a civil war had divided the nation, leaving the northern kingdom of Israel under a growing threat from the Assyrian Empire to the west and north.

The Assyrians had a reputation for being vicious and cruel to those they conquered. In fear and under pressure, many of the people in Israel degenerated spiritually. Under threat, one might think that they would become more faithful to God, more prayerful, more penitent and diligent—but no. Instead, they decided to hedge their bets, so to speak: they might continue to honor their own God, but just in case their God wouldn't help them, they also began to sacrifice to other gods, called Baals, which was about the worst thing they could do. Seeking a second opinion from a doctor may be wise, but seeking a second god is in itself an act of disloyalty, especially since it is against the first two of ten Great Words from that God: "Have no other gods before me," and "Don't make any graven images" (cf. Exod. 20:3–4). Against this backdrop, Hosea's story unfolds.

So Hosea's message from God begins:

> The word of the LORD that came to Hosea son of Beeri during the reigns of Uzziah, Jotham, Ahaz and Hezekiah, kings of Judah, and during the reign of Jeroboam son of Jehoash king of Israel. (1:1 NIV)

Since it is the post–civil war era, Hosea locates himself in terms of the kings of both kingdoms, Israel in the north, Judah in the south.

> When the LORD began to speak through Hosea, the LORD said to him, "Go, take to yourself an adulterous wife and children of unfaithfulness, because the land is guilty of the vilest adultery in departing from the LORD." So he married Gomer daughter of Diblaim, and she conceived and bore him a son. (1:2–3 NIV)

What a stunning prophetic action! Get married and have a family, but be sure to choose an adulterous wife. Through this prophetic action, God evokes the imagery, emotion, and heartbreak of romance, marriage, love, passion, betrayal. Through Hosea's prophetic action, the message would be clear: Israel should be married to the Lord, but she has been flirting unfaithfully with other religions, other gods, other ways of life. Hosea and Gomer marry (through customs far different from our own, no doubt) and have a son, whose naming involves another prophetic action (1:2–5). Chillingly, through the name action, God says, "I will put an end to the kingdom of Israel." The story continues:

> Gomer conceived again and gave birth to a daughter. Then the LORD said to Hosea, "Call her Lo-Ruhamah [= "not loved"], for I will no longer show love to the house of Israel, that I should at all forgive them. Yet I will show love to the house of Judah; and I will save them—not by bow, sword or battle, or by horses and horsemen, but by the LORD their God." (1:6–7 NIV)

So God gives Hosea horrible insight that Israel is doomed, and Judah will be saved, but not by warfare. The naming of his daughter will prophetically dramatize this fact.

> After she had weaned Lo-Ruhamah, Gomer had another son. Then the LORD said, "Call him Lo-Ammi [= "not my people"], for you are not my people, and I am not your God." (1:8–9 NIV)

These are heartbreaking words for the people who carried one of God's names (El) in their name (Isra-el; see Gen. 32:28 NRSV note). But paradoxically, the following lines offer hope:

"Yet the Israelites will be like the sand on the seashore, which cannot be measured or counted. In the place where it was said to them, 'You are not my people,' they will be called 'sons [or 'children,' NRSV] of the living God.' The people of Judah and the people of Israel will be reunited, and they will appoint one leader and will come up out of the land, for great will be the day of Jezreel. Say of your brothers, 'My people,' and of your sisters, 'My loved one.'" (1:10–2:1 NIV)

This kind of prophetic paradox occurs again and again among the Hebrew prophets: there is bad news, really bad news, but then it is to be swallowed up by good news, wonderfully good news. You feel this prophetic paradox in the next part of the drama. At some point Gomer abandons Hosea and their three children, and ultimately she sells herself as a prostitute or sex slave. She finds one man after another ready to take her, use her, compensate her, discard her. Torn by grief, Hosea addresses his three young children, but you realize that, as Hosea's agony erupts, God's grief for his beloved people comes through as well:

> "Rebuke your mother, rebuke her,
>   for she is not my wife,
>   and I am not her husband.
> Let her remove the adulterous look from her face
>   and the unfaithfulness from between her breasts.
> . . . .
> She has not acknowledged that I was the one
>   who gave her the grain, the new wine and oil,
> who lavished on her the silver and gold—
>   which they used for Baal. . . .
> . . . .
> I will punish her for the days
>   she burned incense to the Baals;
> she decked herself with rings and jewelry,
>   and went after her lovers,
>   but me she forgot,"
>   declares the Lord. (2:2, 8, 13 NIV)

"Do you want to understand how God feels about us?" Hosea asks. "Look at me. Think about how I feel after all I've been through. Like me, God is sad, justly angry, devastated, brokenhearted. Like me, God feels the fury of the betrayed." Yet notice what follows. As Hosea listens to God's heart, he hears another message mixed in with the fury and sadness:

> "Therefore I am now going to allure her;
>   I will lead her into the desert
>   and speak tenderly to her.
> There I will give her back her vineyards,
>   and will make the Valley of Achor [= "trouble"] a door
>   of hope.
> There she will sing as in the days of her youth,
>   as in the day she came up out of Egypt." (2:14–15 NIV)

What beautiful words to follow such bitter words! God will take Israel to a kind of second honeymoon. It will be in the desert, a place of aloneness, trial, and reconstruction, and specifically, in the Valley of Achor, the Valley of Trouble, which will become a passageway to hope. The promise continues:

> "In that day," declares the LORD,
>   "you will call me 'my husband';
>   you will no longer call me 'my master.'
> I will remove the names of the Baals from her lips;
>   no longer will their names be invoked.
> In that day I will make a covenant for them
>   with the beasts of the field and the birds of the air
>   and the creatures that move along the ground.
> Bow and sword and battle
>   I will abolish from the land,
>   so that all may lie down in safety.
> I will betroth you to me forever;
>   I will betroth you in righteousness and justice,
>   in love and compassion.
> I will betroth you in faithfulness,
>   and you will acknowledge the LORD.
> . . . .
> I will plant her for myself in the land;
>   I will show my love to the one I called 'Not my loved
>   one.'
> I will say to those called 'Not my people,' 'You are my
>   people';
>   and they will say, 'You are my God.'" (2:16–20, 23 NIV)

So, here are the poignant prophetic words, seething with dramatic tension and profound poetic meaning because they occur in the presence of Hosea's prophetic action. They are words of judgment and mercy, of warning and hope, of fury and tenderness. And they are integrated with this next prophetic action.

> The LORD said to me, "Go, show your love to your wife again, though she is loved by another and is an adulteress. Love her as the LORD loves the Israelites, though they turn to other gods and love the sacred raisin cakes."
>
> So I bought her for fifteen shekels of silver [6 ounces] and about a homer and a lethek [10 bushels] of barley. Then I told her, "You are to live with me many days; you must not be a prostitute or be intimate with any man, and I will live with you." (3:1–3 NIV)

Here the prophetic action concludes. Hosea has displayed God's broken heart for God's unfaithful partner, Israel/Judah, through prophetic action evoking the passion, intensity, love, and fury of a human love affair gone bad. And Hosea has dramatized God's faithful heart in choosing Israel, remaining faithful when Israel was unfaithful, not abandoning her, but buying her back from the sex-slave market after all she had done. She was already his, but he bought her back anyway.

With this example of prophetic action in mind, let's consider Jesus in the role of prophet. Like any prophet, he speaks the word of the Lord in poetic and powerful ways. And he engages in prophetic action as well, actions that are signs (significant) and wonders (making you wonder, or think). He heals blind eyes (dramatizing the blindness of the people at large, their need for healing, and God's desire to heal those with faith), cures lepers and paralytics (with obvious implications about the spiritual and moral condition of the people), turns water at a failed wedding feast into wine (suggesting his power and desire to give "life, life to the full," and the people's need for a profound renewal or reconstitution of their spiritual lives). He feeds multitudes with crumbs (showing that the small beginnings of his movement can have dramatic, global outcomes), turns over the money changers' tables in the temple (dramatizing their for-profit status, in contrast to Jesus's for-prophet status), curses an unfruitful fig tree (a warning to those who bear the name but not the fruit of the faithful), and adds a new level of meaning to the Passover meal ("This bread is my body . . ."). These actions in many ways parallel Hosea's naming of his children: they are significant, and they make people think.

But does any action of Jesus correspond to Hosea's prophetic action of marrying a woman who will break his heart? Do any of his actions show God's heart in this agonizingly tender, vulnerable, yet passionate way?

Could it be that what we call "the passion" is intended as something far more gripping than a cold but necessary legal transaction (which somehow balances an imbalanced equation of justice in the universe)? Could "the passion" of Jesus be, at heart, about something more than or other than an angry God inflicting pain upon an innocent party on behalf of the guilty? Could the cross be a prophetic action proclaiming the horrid ways our stupid, selfish, shortsighted, petty, pathetic, disgusting, ugly sin inflicts pain on the heart of God? On the cross, could Jesus be really and truly revealing the pain of God—God's passionate, poignant, agonizing, sad, longing, dying, loving brokenheartedness for a runaway, beloved creation? Could it be that just as Hosea in a sense exposed God's betrayed heart, Jesus's passion was a prophetic action exposing God as weeping, sweating, bleeding, suffering because of our betrayal? In the passion, could God be saying, not just with Hosea, "You're breaking my heart!" but also through Jesus, "You're torturing me, killing me"?

How different this gripping understanding of the passion of Jesus is from the formulaic transactional understanding promoted by evangelical pop-atonement theology. Just yesterday I was driving in the beautiful Pennsylvania countryside and passed a church with a sign out front that read: WANT TO AVOID BURNING? APPLY SON LOTION. Do you see what this well-intentioned slogan, trying to be cute and clever, unintentionally suggests? First, it compares sin, judgment, and hell to a pesky sunburn. Then, more grossly, it compares Jesus's passion to a cosmetic, a lotion, a minor skin-care product! In so doing, it trivializes the passion of Jesus. How must God feel about that? Is that cute sign itself (symbolic of a view of atonement more widespread than we may wish to admit) a sign of something more—something about us, about our continuing betrayal of God's heart, our ongoing missing of the point that might be funny if it weren't so sick?

Again, remember, prophets use poetic words and prophetic action to get beneath our calloused (and perhaps lotioned?) skin so we don't just superficially understand, but rather so we deeply *feel* and *know*. If Jesus's passion is meant to pierce us on this deeper level, can you see how awful it is if we turn it into something else, something less—whether a suntan lotion or a forensic transaction (glorious in import, to be sure, but forensic nonetheless), a get-out-of-hell-free card, a way of managing a nasty legal problem by striking a deal with the judge?

Think of what Gomer's betrayal said prophetically about the community of faith in Hosea's day. Then ask what the story of the cross as prophetic action says to us about *us*—about our corrupt and betraying religious systems (via the chief priests) that would kill God rather than repent and change; about our political systems (via Pilate and the Romans) that care little for truth and justice, but much for power; about our individual culpability (via Peter) for caring more about our fragile skin than our faithful Friend, or (via Judas) for choosing our own political opinions and financial gain over the Lord; even about our last vestiges of loyalty (via the Marys and the other women), one dim but welcome light on a dark, dark Friday.

Think of what Hosea's enduring love said to his people about God, and then ask what the cross as prophetic action might say to us about God, manifest through "Immanuel, . . . God with us" (Matt. 1:23 NIV). How far will God's love go? The prophetic action of the cross tells us that God's love goes far beyond even Hosea's broken heart, . . . even to Jesus's pierced, tortured body and shed blood and battered, betrayed, emptied spirit. How involved is God in our struggle, our suffering, our pain, our corruption, our oppression, our victimization? When we see the cross as prophetic action, God emerges not as a distant judge transacting legal pardon from a detached distance, but rather as a passionately involved advocate profoundly identified with us, weeping with us in radical empathy, sharing our grief, entering into our shame—God with us, even in suffering and death.

Some of us see this prophetic action on the cross, and we believe not just "it" as an isolated event or concept or message or theory, but even more "him," Jesus—Jesus truly imaging God in word and deed, in sign and wonder, in a manger and in a boat and on a hillside and finally on a cross, always speaking of God.

This way of seeing the cross more fully honors Jesus as Word of God, Word made flesh (cf. John 1:1, 14 KJV), Jesus *speaking God*, not just speaking *of* God or *about* God or *for* God, but *speaking God* in word and deed, the way one speaks English or French. In this view, on the cross Jesus *speaks God*, who loves us with such passion and pain and empathy and desire that no mere words could convey: only a brutal prophetic action could do justice to this speaking.

Some see the same prophetic action, yet they don't believe. They scoff. They see the crucified Jesus as another failed, naive idealist in a long, long, pathetic list. The lesson they take away? Don't take risks. Don't trust God. Don't rock the boat. Don't mess with Caesarly "powers that be" (Rom. 13:1 KJV). It doesn't pay.

Like every prophetic action, then, this one doesn't compel. It doesn't intimidate recalcitrant people into capitulating to a conclusion that they don't believe or want. It says its piece and then withdraws, letting people misinterpret if they will and walk away. But even if they walk away, prophetic action does make them choose how they will interpret the action. They always have a choice, but they don't have a choice about having to make a choice.

Even we who believe have to choose how we will interpret the meaning of the cross. Contemporary pop atonement theology is an interpretation, and therefore a choice, as is this alternate view. Do we choose to see God as the distanced judge, or as the involved victim and friend? Is God the offended potentate who needs somewhere to vent his revenge? Or is God the fellow victim who suffers, endures, accepts the ugliest and fiercest of human rage and injustice—as Hosea suffered and endured Gomer's wandering lusts? Is God the audience waiting for a good performance by Jesus? Or is God-in-Christ the tragic actor, and are we the audience, seeing God pour out his heart, all the while hoping we will truly see, understand, learn, repent, turn, return?[3]

If the cross parallels Gomer's departure and Hosea's pain, how might we interpret the prophetic action of the third day? Doesn't this prophetic action speak with a thousand times the eloquence and volume of Hosea's heroic faithfulness in buying back Gomer, saying that no matter what we do, no matter how we make God suffer, no matter how we reject God, still God will be relentlessly *there*? That we can never escape God, or get rid of God, or kill God off? That even if priests and politicians play wicked power games, even if disciples betray and deny and run, even if fickle crowds praise with palm branches one day and shout "Away with him!" with clenched fists the next, even if humanity shows its most despicable face and twisted heart—even then, God will be there, unmarginalized, undefeated, unstoppable, unavoidable, and undiminished in love for creation? Isn't this an Easter victory that is truly good and saving news, again, news of salvation that forces us, as all prophetic actions must, to choose how we will live?

The more I ponder the cross and resurrection as prophetic action, the more I wonder: What might happen to our understanding of the gospel if we stop theorizing about the cross and resurrection as if they are separated out from the whole dramatic story of Jesus? What would happen to us, instead, if we would learn to take Jesus's birth, life, death, and resurrection together as a unified prophetic word-and-deed, a story that, resonating with Hosea's marriage, shows us a passionate God whose painful faithfulness will never, ever, ever be defeated?

Hosea ends his prophecy with these words, and so will we:

> Who is wise? He will realize these things.
>   Who is discerning? He will understand them.
> The ways of the Lord are right;
>   the righteous walk in them,
>   but the rebellious stumble in them. (14:9 NIV)

Hosea was one of the texts for Rowan Williams's sermon. Brian McLaren, however, has taken a markedly different approach than Williams took. Rather than using life experiences to inform and correct our understanding of a concept, McLaren has used the biblical text to inform and correct our understanding of a concept—prophetic action. I mention this to again highlight the diversity of ways one can appropriately proclaim the scandal of the cross.

Through focusing our attention on the cross and resurrection as prophetic action, McLaren leads us to contemplate something often overlooked: the saving significance of what is revealed through the cross and resurrection. Even if agreeing that transformation of one's view of God through the cross could in fact have salvific import, be life-giving, you might be thinking, "But there is more than that going on at the cross; is this approach adequate?"

If one approaches the atonement from a perspective that there is one correct image or theory, then one would likely not preach a fine sermon like this. If, however, we see the cross and resurrection as having multiple layers of meaning that require multiple images and metaphors to tap and communicate that meaning, that view creates space to make a proclamation like this one. In response to the statement "But there is more than that going on at the cross," one responds, "Yes, certainly."

When McLaren first shared this sermon with me, he expressed concern that it might not be what I was looking for because it used biblical imagery rather than imagery from contemporary life. In fact, I was quite pleased to include this sermon in the book in order to demonstrate that biblical language and images can be used in a contemporary contextual proclamation of the atonement as long as, at key points, they are explained in ways that help listeners in the twenty-first century connect with this language and imagery from another time and place.

To underscore my comments on the appropriateness of diversity of images and approaches, I mention that McLaren uses a quite different approach in his book *The Story We Find Ourselves In*. One of the characters in the book, Neo, roots an explanation of the atonement in a personal experience of betrayal.[4] The contemporary image lends a different character to the presentation. The image itself overlaps with images in this sermon and also communicates other facets of the saving work of the cross.

12

Naked but Unashamed

DOUG FRANK

Brian McLaren urges us to include the cross as prophetic action within the collection of ways we articulate the saving significance of the cross and resurrection. McLaren emphasizes that what we see at the cross has salvific import. In this chapter Doug Frank gives us a powerful example of what McLaren advocated. Frank leads listeners to experience the saving potential of seeing the scandal of Jesus, God incarnate, dying on the cross. In this chapel talk, beautifully contextualized for the evangelical liberal arts college audience, Frank introduces us to the debilitating experience of shame—a theme that will be even more pronounced in the following three chapters.

I went to college in a sleepy town about a half hour's drive from one of the nation's biggest cities. "Thirty minutes from the nearest source of sin," we used to joke. Not exactly a tiny town—thirty thousand people or so, but about as lively as a cemetery. Quiet, shaded streets, solid middle-class houses on comfortable lots. A small business district, two greasy restaurants, assorted parks, libraries, schools. And churches—lots of churches. Traffic was slow, but still there were crossing guards on every corner, mornings and afternoons. People lived in this town because they wanted to be safe. Compared to the bustling city just over the horizon, this town, along with its college, was the very soul of safety.

Funny thing, though—during my four years at this college, I don't remember feeling safe. The trouble started early. As I was moving my luggage into the freshman dorm, the guy across the hall, who had checked in the day before, called me into his room and told me he was a Presbyterian, as if this was the most important thing about him. He asked, "By the way, are you a premillennialist or a postmillennialist?" I gathered from his tone that any freshman worth his salt knew where he stood on this question. I couldn't remember ever having heard these terms, so I put him off with a flippant remark and hurried out to the car for the rest of my luggage. But inside, I felt like an idiot. "What am I doing in college?" I asked myself. I wouldn't know a post-millennialist if he walked up and bit me on the nose. I ought to get back into this car and go home and sell shoes or hamburgers and quit pretending I'm college material.

That encounter set the tone for my next four years. I had some good times in college, moments of warm friendship and high adventure. But mostly, as I think back on those years, I remember how scared I was. I don't think anybody noticed—I was trying rather hard to keep it a secret. I could scarcely admit it to myself. But behind my smiling face lived a timid person for whom a simple walk across campus felt like tiptoeing through a minefield. The prospect of speaking up in class made me tremble: I was sure I'd show myself for a fool. In classes where professors called on people for comment, I sat behind large people and practiced looking inconspicuous. If the professor found me nonetheless, my brain would turn to quartzite, and whatever facts or opinions lodged there became immediately inaccessible.

I was continually aware that I didn't match up to the other students in any of the important categories—clothing or hairstyle or good looks, cool speech and social mannerisms, disposable income, worldly sophistication, intellectual ability. On a couple occasions, I screwed up my courage and invited a girl to a concert or to the only movie allowed on my campus in those days, on the life of Martin Luther. But if she said yes, the evening always produced enough moments of excruciating embarrassment, for some faux pas that I had committed, or imagined I had committed, that I'd give up women for the foreseeable future.

I did make a few male friends at college—at least, I got to know a few guys well enough that we spent many hours hanging out, eating pizza and playing cards, cramming for exams, mocking chapel speakers, rating women, and discussing big questions late into the night, quite sure that we were breaking new philosophical ground. (I finally figured out what a postmillennialist was.) But even as "best friends," we kept most of how we felt about ourselves a secret. Hardly ever did we share our deepest fears or embarrassment or sadness or confusion. I don't remember any of us admitting to being hurt when another person in the group made a cruel remark about us. Mostly, we showed one another the cool confidence of someone who thinks he's OK. If we didn't feel OK, we didn't feel safe enough to say so out loud.

Is my experience typical of college students, in those days or today? Back then, I would have said no. I would never have guessed that I was typical. I was quite sure I was the only person who felt this flawed and fearful inside. That's what shame is about: it always singles you out as uniquely damaged goods. And your shame is one of the things you're ashamed of, so you never tell anyone else how you feel about yourself, and you never have the chance to hear that they feel the same way.

As I've grown older, I've begun to suspect that many of us do feel the same way. One clue has come from noticing how often other people seem taken in by my normal disguises. When I mention to someone how unsafe I feel in a particular situation, how nervous I am before giving a public talk, or how shy I feel with strangers, they are usually surprised. *They* feel that way, but they can't imagine that I do. "You're so relaxed and confident and comfortable in your skin," they say. "Well, yes," I tell them. "That's my disguise. I've practiced it for years." And then I realize that maybe that's what we were all doing in college, practicing our disguises, even those students who to my eyes appeared to be so relaxed and confident and comfortable in their skins. Maybe, inside, they felt scared and ridiculous too.

Here's another clue. For the last thirty years, in a small community amid the southern Oregon mountains, I've taught college students in a nontraditional academic program. Every fall our students arrive, several dozen of them, looking, one might say, bright-eyed and bushy tailed. They have big plans: they're going to hit the books, think profound thoughts, talk about the big ideas. Most of them seem at ease with themselves and happy to be who they are.

The first night we sit in a circle in front of a big stone fireplace and introduce ourselves. It's an awkward time—a bunch of strangers trying to make a good impression. Some try to be funny, some mysterious. Some regale us with their summer's exploits; some outline a series of impressive-sounding goals for the semester. A few are content to say little. The masks many of them are wearing often say something like this: "I'm a relatively bright and capable person, maybe just a tiny bit brighter and more capable than you, but I'm also a nice person, so I won't rub it in. I can see that I'm going to like it here, and you're going to like me, and isn't life in the mountains going to be wonderful? What a safe place to be for a semester!"

But that's only the first night. And those are the masks. By the third or fourth week, and sometimes sooner, the masks are coming off. We're starting to trust one another, and we're ready to say more of the truth about ourselves. In moments of honesty, we often hear a different tune: "That first night we were here, and we went around the circle introducing ourselves? I felt like the biggest fool. How did I get myself into this? Listen to these folks talk: they all sound so mature and experienced and talented. I'm a dunce in a group of geniuses. An imposter. By the end of the first small-group discussion, everybody here is going to know I'm a moron. How can I get out of this place without embarrassing myself?" This testimony comes as much from the students who, on the first night, were the most intimidatingly smooth and profound, as it does from those who showed their nervousness more openly.

I wonder if it is not nearly universal that, in varying degrees, we experience the world as an unsafe place, a place where we cannot really be ourselves, cannot be confident that we are acceptable, that others will love us, no matter what. I would hazard a guess that inside most of us, in relative measures, hides a person who feels small, perhaps pathetic or ridiculous or confused or inadequate, and often rather scared. Most of us learn to adjust to this painful reality so well, perhaps, that we go through our days without focusing on the inner landscape, almost forgetting it. And to keep it from others, we each seem drawn to our own set of disguises.

Some of us come off as particularly powerful or successful or confident. We make good grades, perform well in sports or music, talk a good line, wear the right clothes, hang out with the right friends, wear a practiced smile on our faces. Others use less obvious ploys, such as silence or anger or cynicism or physical isolation, to keep others from seeing how bad we feel about ourselves. But secretly, don't we often feel that we're fundamentally deficient as human beings? Aren't we careful not to be exposed, in all our ridiculousness, for all the world to see? Isn't this a sign that, for most of us, the world is not really a safe place?

Where does this stuff come from? Well, if you think about it, the world *is*, in some ways, a dangerous place. Fear seems built into the animal world. Evolutionary biologists think fear is what fuels the struggle to survive; they suggest that animals with more highly honed fear instincts have more successfully adapted to the dog-eat-dogginess of the natural world. Where I live, I often watch deer in their natural habitat. What strikes me is their perpetually keen state of alertness. A deer will bend over to get a mouthful of grass, but not for long. It will look up quickly and often and start at the slightest noise. It seems like the most jumpy, nervous animal in the world. It's probably still alive, munching away in the woods, *because* it's been nervous; otherwise, one of our local mountain lions would long ago have made a tasty lunch out of it. For animals who live in an unsafe world, who can be hurt and die, fear seems to be a necessary tool for survival.

As little kids, we were perhaps not that different. We were tender little things with a growing self-consciousness and easily bruised egos, so we could be hurt in many more ways than could a deer. We needed to survive, not just physically but also emotionally. It's as if we came into the world with a question on our minds—not one we could put into words, but one we could *feel* inside us: "Is this world a safe place for me to be *me*? If I am *me*, will I be taken care of, accepted, affirmed, loved? If I am *me*, will people honor me and treat me with respect?"

Parents have the awesome responsibility of trying to make the world safe for the child to become authentically oneself. They do this by taking the child's needs seriously, by *being there* with a gentle and loving response. This is a daunting, tiring task, even for those parents whose own childhood needs were so well met that they instinctively know how to be attuned to their child's needs. Yet the most caring parents fail in countless small ways. And self-denigrating or angry or anxious or perfectionistic and controlling parents—parents like me, in other words—fail in countless bigger ways.

Sudden bursts of anger at a young child can make the child feel extremely bad deep down, and continual doses of this treatment will lay the foundation for a sense of shame that can last a lifetime. A parent who ignores the child, or laughs at the child, or criticizes the child, gives the child the impression that, at the very core, one is fundamentally deficient or ridiculous. These sudden ruptures in the safety of parent-child relationships teach the child that it's not a safe world in which to *be oneself*—to feel what one feels, to need what one needs—and the child begins to operate out of a fear that if the inner self is exposed, one will lose the love of the people who count most.

It would be nice to think that Christian families are immune to these human problems. But no families are immune. In fact, Christian families, for all their good intentions and sincere love, often make their children's world an even more dangerous place to be, even when they are trying to do the opposite. The twenty-first-century world is rife with dangers to body and soul. Teen culture, in particular, offers infinite paths to ruin. Christian parents work harder than most to make sure their kids stay *good*, build *character*, know the difference between *right and wrong*, and have what it takes to do the right. In their anxiety and with the best intentions, they often are excessively controlling. They moralize and scrutinize, evaluate and judge.

If we come from families like this, we may feel the *pressure to be good* but never the *freedom to be ourselves*. We may learn that appearance—the appearance of good behavior or deep faith, for example—is what will gain the approval of others. If we internalize these controls, we may even try to make sure we *feel* the right thing—that we feel loving toward our little brother when actually, at this moment, we hate him; that we stop feeling angry or hurt when we have good reason to be angry or hurt. We are uncomfortable with our truest feelings: they seem bad and seem to threaten the love we need from others. So we hide what we really feel, from others and most harmfully, from ourselves. We carry a zone of danger around inside us and feel unsafe even in the most benign circumstances.

Many of us, in effect, are living under the constant scrutiny of an *unkindly eye*. We have this vague, continuing awareness that someone is watching us, and it feels as if the eye that's watching is the eye of an enemy: someone who laughs at us, or dislikes us, or criticizes us mercilessly. When we are children, this is the eye, mainly, of our parents when they are disapproving. As teens, it is often the eye of our peers, whom we imagine are looking at us with disdain. As college students, perhaps it's the eye of a teacher who is scrutinizing us with an unfriendly gaze. And as Christians, tragically I think, many of us experience God as one really big, often critical and unkindly Eye.

Quite a few years ago now, I came to the realization that I didn't like God. This was a surprise to me. I had been a Christian since I gave my life to Jesus as a seven-year-old. I had sung hymns, memorized Bible verses, prayed prayers, all attesting to my love for God and for his Son Jesus. I could say without conscious deceit, but also without thinking much about it, that I loved God. But when I focused on my actual experience of God, I noticed a discomfort with God that lurked around the edges of my so-called "love": I realized that I didn't actually feel close to God. For years—when I tried to read the Bible, for example, or listened to sermons or tried to pray without making any real contact—I had, without consciously admitting it, felt ambivalent and confused about God, and quite far away from God. It seemed an important discovery at the time, one I had been unconsciously putting off. I didn't like the kind of person God was, and although I admired his perfect Son Jesus, I didn't really like him either. I didn't like them because I didn't feel safe with them.

Since that moment of recognition, I've thought a lot about my relationship with God. I think my discomfort with God started quite early, when I experienced God as the kind of person whose love is conditional and controlling. My good Christian parents and a lot of other good Christian people had depicted God as mainly interested in making me good. "Remember, God is watching you at all times," they would say. "Don't do anything Jesus wouldn't do, don't go anywhere Jesus wouldn't go, don't feel anything Jesus wouldn't feel." It seemed as if God didn't like who I really was. God liked his idea of the perfect Doug, which looked a lot like a perfect Jesus. I couldn't be the perfect Doug *or* the perfect Jesus. No wonder I didn't like God: God didn't like me. As I imagined God's eyes on me, I felt ashamed.

Like most of you, my elders always told me that God loved me, which is why it took me so long to figure this stuff out. But now I can see that the way they described God's love was itself confusing. God loved me so much, they taught me, that he gave his only Son Jesus to die for my sins. My sins were bad in God's eyes, so bad that I deserved to suffer forever in hell. But God sent Jesus to suffer in my place, and this satisfied God's requirement that a penalty be paid before God could welcome me into his family and take me to heaven when I died. When I was still a child, this story sounded reasonable enough. My parents seemed to think that bad deeds deserved punishment, so it made sense that God would too. But as I grew older and started thinking about this story and reading more about Jesus, I became uneasy with the God this story depicted.

Does this God need to hurt somebody before he can draw close to me? Why can't God just forgive me, as Jesus asked his disciples to forgive *their* enemies without extracting a penalty, or as Jesus himself forgave his killers from the cross they put him on, even though they hadn't asked to be forgiven? My teachers said that God couldn't do that because of the strict standards of his justice, which requires a penalty. But a God who kills somebody out of loyalty to an abstract principle doesn't feel truly loving either. And the God in this story seemed so demanding: for my childish sins, would he abandon me forever in a place of excruciating torture? Isn't this penalty a little disproportionate to my offense? This doesn't sound like love. I couldn't imagine my own father sending me to hell forever, no matter how badly I had offended him. Isn't God's love at least as forgiving and long-suffering as the love of my parents?

I labored to believe in God's love, which others taught me with such certainty, and to love God in return. But after many years of trying, I had to confess that I had failed. For the record I could say that I loved God, but I didn't really like God very much, and I didn't think God liked me either. Aside from a few emotionally charged moments, under the influence of charismatic preachers or teachers, I felt distant from God. When I read the Bible, I felt scrutinized by the big unfriendly Eye. It was hard to admit this, even to myself. After all, if the Big Eye sensed my dislike, wouldn't I be doubly condemned. But deep inside, I *felt* unloved by God, *felt* that in order to earn this God's approval I would need to be something I was not, and perhaps could never be. The God who killed his Son for my sins did not feel like a safe God.

Over the last several decades of my life, things have changed for me. My admission that I did not like or trust God was a moment of truth that turned me in a quite different direction on my spiritual journey. The journey has been winding and sometimes difficult. But it has left me with a conviction that is as deep in me as anything I know or believe. I am now quite sure that the God of the Big Eye is a bogus God. He is not, and has never been, truly the God of Abraham, Isaac, and Jacob. He is not the God of Paul, the writer of so much of our New Testament. He is not the God of Jesus. The God of the Big Eye, I am quite sure, is a God that human beings have made up, a God as false and as harmful as any of the idols the Old Testament prophets railed against. How have we come to do this—to make up a God who so often feels like our enemy, and then try to love him?

Perhaps it was inevitable—given the anxiety of human life, the fragility of human love, the disease of self-accusation, of feeling small and helpless and ridiculous, of scrutinizing ourselves critically and rejecting who we think we are at the core—inevitable that we would project these same feelings onto God. Perhaps the process of imagining a demanding and judgmental God is quite similar to the process of imagining, in our embarrassment and shame, that the people around us have unkindly eyes toward us, even when they may only wish us well. Maybe that's what the story in Genesis is trying to teach when it tells us that Adam and Eve covered themselves in the Garden of Eden. It seems that, invariably, humans project onto God their own self-contempt, and then they suffer in the unkindly gaze of this unlovable, imaginary God.

I know this will be hard for some of you to hear, as for many years it was hard for me to hear. Our picture of God is deep in our brains, deep in our guts. We have heard countless Bible stories—particularly from the Old Testament—to support this God of the Big Unkindly Eye; countless Sunday school lessons to remind us that God knows our every move; and probably more than a few sermons on the terrors of hell reserved for those whom God finds wanting. We cannot believe that we can interpret the texts behind such stories in any other way than the one in which we heard it. I confess to believing that every one of those texts has been torn from its context, misinterpreted, and misused to depict a God whom Jesus would not recognize as the one he called his Father.

Then who is the God whom Jesus came to reveal? Strangely, I have met this God in the one who died, forgiving his enemies, on a cross two thousand years ago. But it is a cross that symbolizes something quite different from a tool God used to punish his perfect Son for my sins. That teaching has dominated the church's view of the atonement for almost a thousand years, and that is long enough. The one I see on the cross, in his broken body, reveals a surprising truth about the way God really is. This Jesus hangs there in a most ungodly pose—naked, bound, wounded, exposed to our contempt—and yet compassionate toward those who hung him there. Does genuine faith begin in the moment of shock, when we realize that the God who broods invisibly over the earth is not a figure of power and glory and majesty, at least as we normally define these terms? That God is rather more truly present to us as one who is vulnerable, seemingly powerless, and infinitely forgiving?

To the eyes of faith, the crucifixion bears witness to an unconventional, almost unbelievable God. Here is not the distant God of the philosophers, not the oversized and demanding God of every human religion, including what passes for Christian religion. Instead, we see a God who has endured our rejection from the beginning of human time, who has refused and still refuses to treat our rejection as final. From the foundation of the earth, this God has hung, crucified and willingly powerless, subjected to our misunderstanding and our rejection, waiting, loving, imploring us to recognize how radically this God is *for us*. Imploring us to recognize that even at our worst, God will be present to us in compassion, so that nothing we do or think or feel, in life or in death, can separate us from the love of God.

In this safety there is salvation for the anxious, self-doubting, self-accusing person that I am. The cross exposes God's Unkindly Eye as a fiction. In Jesus, God comes to me as a brother who knows me in the deepest possible way, who loves me unfailingly, who likes and celebrates the person I am and wants only for me to become more and more fully myself. But this is only the beginning of salvation. Because the sad truth is that if God and every other human being ceased this moment to scrutinize me with an unkindly eye, I would not yet be free of my own unkindly eye. I need a new relationship with myself as much as I need a new relationship with God. And this too begins on the cross.

What we have learned to be ashamed of in ourselves—our fear and helplessness and vulnerability—Jesus displayed openly at Calvary. The nakedness that symbolizes our ridiculous humanity, which we work so hard to hide both figuratively and literally, Jesus willingly embodied before our eyes, "despising the shame" of it (Heb. 12:2 RSV). When Jesus's enemies poured their contempt on him, were they not simply displacing onto his naked human flesh the contempt they felt for their own human flesh? It is not hard to believe that this self-contempt, this shame that we take so deeply into ourselves from our earliest experience, is the source of every unloving act in the world, and thus the root cause of all that the Bible calls sin.

I believe it is the task of the Spirit of God to save us from *this* sin, this utter self-alienation, by giving us new eyes for the cross. In the dying Jesus, we see not only a human God. We also see Jesus revealing to us *our own human selves* without disguise. It is the Spirit's doing, I believe, if at this moment of recognition, for perhaps the first time in our lives, we respond with compassion instead of contempt. Our hearts melt with love for the sad, lonely, hurting person that has lived inside us and, like God, has endured our rejection for as long as we can remember. We recognize the accusing eye as the understandable product of our own fears, and in the exhilaration from a new sense of safety, our fears lose much of their power. We hear a helpless, human God say these liberating words: "Here I am, willing to be who I really am, but also who *you* really are. Now, why don't *you* be willing to be you? Why don't you allow *yourself* to become fully human—to feel helpless and lost and bleeding, and *not ashamed*? It's OK to feel the same compassion for your own deepest, truest self as God feels for that self. It's OK to be *you*.

This salvation—a reunification with all that is in us, in others, and in God—sets radical changes in motion in our lives.

We become freer to feel and to confess our own pain, our own fear, our own helplessness. Shame loosens its hold on us, and we begin to wear our nakedness more openly. Others experience us as safer, so they become more honest about themselves, and our relationships become more authentic than they were when we were all hiding behind our impressive disguises. In these vital reconnections—with ourselves, with others, and with God—we feel more fully ourselves, more alive. Isn't this the joyful news that Jesus's resurrection announces? The way of the cross—this embrace of our own vulnerability and weakness and pain, which to us so often feels like death itself—is actually the way to life.

When the apostle Paul wrote to the Corinthian church about the cross, he reminded them of the foolishness of it all, or as he put it, its scandal. How can the abject weakness and patent foolishness of a dying God be the source of our salvation? And yet, he said, for those who believe, it does become just that. I am one of those who believe. For me, the cross has become a kind of mirror. In its reflection I see myself as I am when I am free to inhabit my full humanity: wounded, weakened, but unashamed and loving toward my enemies as I am toward myself. But the face reflected in this mirror is not only mine. It is also God's. It is the wounded face of a God who, as Immanuel, is one with me in my suffering and shows me the part of God that is broken so that I can be fully reconciled with the part of me that is broken. When in the mirror of the cross I can see God's face, my neighbor's face, *and* my own face—all three at once—I know what it means that God is closer to me than I am to myself. And in that moment, I am finally safe.

This is the good news: since God is so wildly and scandalously for us, who, including ourselves, can possibly be against us?

In this chapel talk Frank powerfully and graphically communicates the saving significance of the cross as revelation—both the revelation of a God fundamentally different from the God of the unkindly eye he experienced as a youth, and through Jesus the revelation of an authentic human being. Frank aptly communicates the transformational potential of this dual revelation at the cross in a contextually appropriate way. If he presented this as the single explanation of the atoning work of the cross, I could critique it for what is left out. Instead, however, I celebrate that acknowledging the need to use diverse and multiple images of the atonement to capture the full saving significance of the cross and resurrection creates space for a presentation like this one. If we limit our atonement proclamation to one image, we lose the full revelatory significance of the cross.

13

The Family Table

GRACE Y. MAY

In the following autobiographical presentation to Chinese-Americans, Grace May uses contrasting images of the family table to proclaim the potential of the cross and resurrection of Jesus Christ to transform our relationship with God, ourselves, and others. She relates the atonement directly to her own and her audience's experience of shame. May also proclaims other facets of the atoning work of the cross and resurrection in this multilayered work, which well exemplifies the biblical model of contextualizing the gospel that connects with yet also challenges the audience's culture.

Every night as a child, I watched as our conversations around the dinner table disintegrated into disputes. Frustrations at work, weariness from a long commute, a hankering for a better life, differences in my parents' attitude toward God, even a distaste for the food—any of these could trigger the exchange of disparaging words. Inevitably the meal ended with my father announcing his need for a divorce.

Our family troubles seemed to tarnish our civilization's untainted three-thousand-year record of strong and stable families. After all, we were *Chinese*, and the assumption is that Chinese have intact families. But after hearing one tragic story after another, I have concluded that healthy Chinese families tend to be the exception rather than the rule. In the United States, adjusting to life as an immigrant saddles many families with more stress than we can handle, but the only safe place most of us feel comfortable enough for expressing raw emotions is at home. Consequently, pent-up anger, humiliation, and rage erupt in the confines of our home.

Internecine battles, however, are not new to our collective history. Although we might not be aware of the more blemished chapters of our history, a realistic account cannot ignore them. In ancient China men, from the emperor down to the farmer, prided themselves on having more than one wife and having several concubines. Having multiple partners represented status, wealth, and male prerogative. Men routinely set aside their wives when they could not produce male heirs. Women took their own lives when they could no longer bear the scorn of spiteful second, third, and fourth wives. Far from engendering harmony, multiple generations living under one roof led to family discord, backbiting, and bitterness. Jealousy, weeping, and gnashing of teeth fill Chinese lore and history.

Nevertheless, the media typically hail Chinese-Americans as the model minority. Could it be, though, that we have earned the epithet as much by our acquiescence to authority as by our accomplishments? Afraid of creating waves, we have learned not to complain. Instead of disturbing the dominant culture's perceptions, we have chosen, for the most part, to endure silently. In the mid- to late 1800s, when our forebears first arrived on the East and West Coasts, we served almost exclusively as waiters, cooks, laundry workers, and domestics. Then, society labeled us as bad for the economy and treated us as ignorant coolie labor, confining many of us to residences in Chinatown and limiting our participation in politics. White paranoia led to talk of the yellow peril, propaganda that accused Chinese of stealing jobs from red-blooded Americans. During the gold rush and the building of the first transcontinental railroad, instead of shrugging off the inappropriate shame of our past, we swallowed our pain.

The Chinese term for "suffering" graphically captures the sense. *Chi ku* literally means "to eat bitterness."

During the last century the history of China has compounded the sense of toxic shame. Beginning with the Opium Wars of the mid-nineteenth century, China has endured abject poverty, Western and Japanese imperialism, famine, drought, flooding, civil war, political chaos, and social upheaval. Natural catastrophes, wars, and revolution have devastated the land and traumatized the family, causing many to flee to other countries. In America, the immigrant experience, while providing opportunities, has also taken its toll on the family. In light of the Confucian ideal of cultivating scholar-sages, parents have denied themselves in order to provide their children with every educational and material advantage.

Unfortunately for many second-generation Chinese-Americans, the push for success has translated into strain. By equating personal worth with productivity, we measure our success by our earnings and our clockable hours. With the constant reinforcement of the media, we have come to believe that we are self-made. Consciously or unconsciously, we have absorbed our parents' immigrant mind-set that we have achieved everything on our own—our status, our money, our careers, our families, and our happiness. Why would we of all people need a savior? Materialism, an inflated sense of self, and faulty definitions of success have blinded us to our need for God and every human being's need for God.

Human greed and our consumer mentality only aggravate the problem and feed our voracious appetite for more. We stockpile degrees and dollars. We hold our possessions close to our hearts. We receive applause, but still long for others to affirm us as people rather than producers. To avoid confronting the root cause of our pain and sense of inadequacy, we distract ourselves. We pour ourselves into senseless activities instead of evaluating the merits of other people's estimation of ourselves. We squander our money on shopping, gambling, and entertainment. We engage in illicit sex and find ourselves sinking into a deeper and deeper quagmire of sin, mainly because we cannot shake off the inappropriate shame we do not have to bear. Then we spin our wheels, denying that we are living a lie or misspending. We rationalize our needs, seeking refuge in the suburbs, and fleeing into our private worlds—all the while ignoring the wider needs of the kingdom of God and keeping a safe distance from neighbors who could actually hold us accountable.

But what would happen if, instead of yielding to our cultural tendency to save face, we looked to Jesus and openly confessed our mistakes? I imagine, more times than not, that our eyes would meet the eyes of a merciful Savior, who chose to be mocked and scorned for our sakes, taking on our shame, so that we could walk with our heads raised up again. How much freer and more vulnerable we would allow ourselves to be if at the core of our being we knew that God accepted us and that we could bless others, not in spite of our weakness, but *in* our weakness? Open confession allows us to identify and empathize with our neighbors and them with us. What we risk by exposing our weaknesses and losing face, we gain by underscoring our common denominator with the world: our neediness. And our Redeemer delights in few things more than in restoring our freedom to be truly ourselves.

> In you our ancestors trusted;
>   they trusted, and you delivered them.
> To you they cried, and were saved;
>   in you they trusted, and were not put to shame.
>   (Ps. 22:4–5 NRSV)

My mother embodies for me the power of the cross and the resurrection. She came to America and later married my father. After becoming a Christian, my mother spoke of God often and expressed concern for my father's spiritual well-being. My father responded with annoyance and occasionally with violence. Once my father threw a knife at her; it changed direction in midair and landed with the tip embedded in the breakfast table. Another time he threw a wrench at her; it passed within inches of her head, leaving a hole in the wall. The wrench came so close that under her breath she asked God to receive her life. Yet whenever I hear my mother share her testimony, in her voice I detect not shame but gratitude. She is grateful for God's faithfulness in preserving her life and giving her a story to tell. In her own way, she has subverted our culture's priority on saving face by making her broken marriage a showcase of God's grace. She is Exhibit A in God's courtroom.

In sharp contrast, I grew up shunning the topic of my parents' divorce. I was loath to admit that my father had abandoned us and would have much preferred attributing the divorce to "irreconcilable differences" than hearing from my mother's own lips that my father had walked out on us. I could never understand why my mother would want to tell anyone about my father's attacks or flare-ups. To my knowledge, no one else in our Chinese church suffered from domestic violence, so why draw attention to ourselves? For me, the fewer people who knew about our family, the better, because I wanted to conceal our shame.

Ironically, at the private school I attended, I did not feel any need to conceal my parents' marital status, because fully half of my classmates also came from divorced families. But what did make me feel self-conscious was my mother's employment. Most of my classmates' families hired help to do the house chores, while my mother served as a live-in housekeeper. I was embarrassed. I kept feeling a nagging sense of want. No matter how much attention I received, I always wanted more.

Similarly, no matter how many times I heard that God's grace was free, I could not conceive of a love that came without strings attached. Consequently, I tried to earn what I could have received only as a gift. Perfectionism drove me to panic before tests, pull all-nighters, and covet A's. Instead of treasuring friendships as gifts from God, I sought to win people's affection. Then, after I had gained the trust of a friend, I would sabotage the relationship. I repeated the pattern ad nauseum. Lonely, discontent, and restless, I would have continued down a never-ending spiral except that God intervened.

As a teenager, I began to experience God's love more deeply. After hearing a sermon or a Sunday school lesson, I often found myself shedding tears, wondering how God knew exactly what I needed to hear. At retreats, God found a special way to my heart through the fellowship, messages, and testimonies. To this day, I remember staring at Christ's body hanging on a cross with his head bowed as our youth counselor spoke about the pain we inflicted on Christ every time we sinned. I never enjoyed guilt trips, but whenever I looked Jesus squarely in the face, my rebelliousness melted, and the depths of Jesus's love and agony swallowed up my reluctance to confront myself. For even at his moment of greatest defeat, with his hands tied, Christ conquered my shame. He freed me from the shame that I suffered because of the pain I inflicted on others. Instead of my hands, I saw my Savior's hands, nail-pierced, hanging from the cross. My sin met its match in the cross. Christ won decisively in two arenas. He delivered me from guilt (the dreadful weight of my conscience) and released me from despair (the fear that I would always succumb to old ways).

Perfect love casts out fear. (1 John 4:18 NRSV)

Although my experiences in the Chinese church gave me a profound sense of my need for cleansing and forgiveness, my five years in the African-American church gave me a taste of God's incomparable joy and power. On Sundays at Roxbury Presbyterian Church, passing the peace took ten minutes as people walked around the pews, giving one another hugs and greetings. The warm physical embrace made me feel accepted even before people had checked my résumé or knew my name. I also discovered that whatever mood I was in, my feelings never presented a barrier too high for God. If I was down, God picked me up with both hands. If I was happy, God pushed me over the top. Over and over, God demonstrated his power to heal and to raise up.

God's presence was undeniable especially during communion services. "If you feel unworthy," the pastor said, "then this table is for you." His words seemed like the reverse of everything I had previously learned in church, that those who are unworthy should abstain, with an emphasis on our unworthiness. Yet my journey had taught me that it was precisely the awareness of my need for God that prompted God to respond. Jesus had set the table, knowing full well who I was, and he still welcomed me. So instead of focusing on my inadequacies and shame, I rejoiced that God had made a place for me—not because of anything I had done or not done, but because of Christ's power to include me in the family and make my place secure. And what's more, God did not bypass my feelings either. As brothers and sisters sang, "Let us break bread together on our knees," I accepted the invitation to share in their singing and to join in God's grace. In the eating and the drinking, it was as if God led me through a window in the cross that opened up to the resurrection.

> Jesus on the night when he was betrayed took a loaf of
>   bread,
> and when he had given thanks, he broke it and said,
> "This is my body that is broken for you." (1 Cor. 11:23–24
>   NRSV with note)

It was nightfall when Jesus and his disciples were sitting at the table and eating. Jesus interrupted his friends' bickering and vying for greatness and gave them an object lesson about sacrifice. Breaking a piece of bread and pouring out some wine, he gave them his body and his blood. It was a poignant moment, but one that may have gotten lost in the disciples' shock, stares, and murmurings. While the disciples wondered who was going to betray Jesus, the larger question remained unanswered: will redemption, as God conceived it, work? How else can we explain the intense struggle that ensued when Jesus pleaded with the Father to remove the cup from him? Still, God's grace prevailed.

My parents never did reconcile. Their divorce left splinters in my life. I reacted and lodged my own thorns in their lives and others' lives. I felt desperate and afraid, wanting to stop the cycle of hurt but always finding myself trapped in it again. But God never abandoned me. On the contrary, God pursued me and spoke my language of love. God gave me friends who both gave me room to grow and tenaciously held on to me, prayers that lifted me up and out of myself, words that encouraged and affirmed me, and worship that helped me to experience God's presence. Wave after wave of grace and mercy began to convince me that Christ's way works. Every time the body splinters or suffers a stab, there *is* the possibility for healing and repair. And every time people repent, the Spirit ignites the atoning work of Christ anew.

God had an answer to my shame and guilt and named him Jesus.

When we sin, God does not flatter us. God compares us to a naked, used whore. Yet while we are still filthy, God pleads with open arms for us to come back. Not afraid of being contaminated, Christ comes to us, wanting to hold us, bathe us, and clothe us. And no matter how pathetic and stubborn we may be, God's cry remains, "Come back."

Other times, we are so hurt and so angry that we lash out at others. Kicking and screaming, we attack those who love us the most. We flail around in our helplessness and despair. Yet Christ still seeks us. His love makes him bold and impervious to our cries to be left alone. Taking the place of our enemy on the cross, Christ pleads, "Hit me." He wants us to strike him and not another. For he alone can absorb the hate and break the cycle of violence.

Our pain is real, but so are the cries of the Lamb. The truth is that we have all been hit and spat upon; we have all hurt and mocked others. But only the lashes on Christ's back carry the power to heal and forgive. Nothing else can stop the aching or the throbbing. No other power can remove our need to strike back. Christ offers forgiveness after we have cast the first stone, offering reconciliation to two parties that abhor each other. Moreover, Christ is the scapegoat that bears away all our shame, absorbing the voices that tell us we are of no value or consequence. In his body he bears all the insults and hostilities we have borne.

How does God save? By keeping his covenant oath to love us whatever the cost.

Only the truth of the atonement can cut through the dichotomy of our inner and outer states. Only the brutality of the cross and the compassion of Christ can bestow the acceptance that we crave and permit us to be our real selves. Only Christ's broken body can absorb the pain, the suffering, the injustice, and the indignities of all people. By abandoning status, riches, and strength, Christ in his humility and humiliation frees us from our sense of inadequacy and hesitations to proclaim the message of redemption. We readily concede that the triumph of the cross differs from the path of victory that most of us would chart; but then, the battle is not ours but the Lord's.

Relieved and grateful, we can shed tears of joy over God's grace, not tears of self-pity. For the resurrection tells us that our restoration is in sight. Soon our relationship with God and with one another and with the entire cosmos will be restored. On that grand day, we will no longer be foreigners or aliens, but full-fledged citizens. No more hiding and striving. All our scars and old scores will be put away. Christ will welcome us, rejoicing and exulting over the one whom he has wooed and waited for so patiently to arrive . . . home. Clothed in sparkling, white garments, we will worship the One who gave himself for us and cleansed us by his blood. Then we will joyfully take our seats at the banqueting table, eating, drinking, and reveling as only family can. Amen.

———

Grace May clearly communicates her culture's drive to save face and avoid shame, as well as the shame she experienced because of her family situation. Against all odds her mother learned to live free from shame, and May has come to experience that liberation as well.

Although many portrayals of the cross focus on the physical suffering, May's presentation places more stress on the shame of the cross. This emphasis communicates to May's readers the reality that in their experience of shame, God in Jesus has fully identified with them and has experienced the shameful exclusion they fear. Not only did Jesus know shame; he also stood in solidarity with the shamed and excluded of his day, which contributed to his being rejected and killed on the cross. The cross, however, offers more than a promise of God's solidarity and God's knowing what it means to experience shame.

The cross exposes false shame and breaks its power to instill fear. On the cross Jesus was inappropriately shamed, and the cross and resurrection exposed the lie. The cross exposed, or shamed, the powers that falsely shamed Jesus (Col. 2:15). Jesus's death and resurrection invite and enable us to live in freedom from this dehumanizing shame that he despised and disregarded on the cross (Heb. 12:2). At the same time, however, there is appropriate shame. There are things for which humans should feel shame. The most shameful act in history was crucifying God incarnate. Those who sought to shame Jesus were in fact those who acted shamefully. Shame alienates and destroys relationships, but on the cross and after the resurrection Jesus responded with relationship-restoring acts of forgiveness and acceptance. God removes the alienation of shame through love. In exposing the misplaced shame and lovingly revealing the true failure of us all, Jesus, the "friend of sinners," removed the stigma and hostility that alienates us from each other and God.

The gospel does not dissipate or heal shame in the same way as guilt because guilt focuses on an action and shame on the self. Guilt is linked to fears of punishment for a misdeed; shame is linked to fears of rejection and exclusion for falling short of societal expectations. Punishment will alleviate guilt but will not remove shame. Love banishes shame. Throughout May's work we see the relational element in the atoning work of the cross and resurrection, as in her central image of the family table. She was freed from her shame in a deep and profound way through her experience of communion at Roxbury Presbyterian Church, where "in the eating and the drinking, it was as if God led me through a window in the cross that opened up to the resurrection." The proclamation and celebration of the Lord's death and resurrection release the powerful current of God's love and acceptance. The embrace and joy shared by members of the body of Christ joined around the table continue in an ongoing way in the life of the body.[1]

The testimonial nature of May's message highlights the need for us to enter into Christ's healing and atoning love. It demonstrates the reality that it is not only possible for us to use various images to proclaim the saving significance of the cross and resurrection; it is also necessary because we need all the facets of salvation offered through the cross. For instance, although May focused on shame, she also shared how she experienced release from guilt. In her powerfully concrete final section, she not only presents Jesus as a substitute who bears our shame. Jesus also takes the place of our enemies, breaking the cycle of violence by absorbing the insults and blows we would like to heap upon those who have offended and hurt us. Through Christ's sacrificial death we are reconciled and brought to the table together.

14

Jesus, the Ultimate Outsider

MIKE MCNICHOLS

In the previous chapter Grace May roots her proclamation of the saving significance of the cross and resurrection in her culture's focus on saving face and avoiding shame. To say, however, that some cultures are more shame oriented and others more guilt oriented does not mean that the former does not experience the burden of guilt nor that the latter does not experience debilitating shame. The Bible presents the work of the cross as providing freedom from both, and we would do well to not limit ourselves only to images of salvation from guilt or only to images of salvation from shame. In the following sermon Mike McNichols provides us with an excellent example of addressing the issue of shame in a way that connects with an audience in a cultural context more typically described as "guilt based," where one would more commonly hear the cross related to the problem of guilt. He preached this sermon on Sunday, April 1, 2001, at Soulfarers Community, a Vineyard Church thirty-five miles east of Los Angeles in Fullerton, California.

Today is the fifth Sunday of Lent. During this season of the church year, we've been considering what it means to stand before God as ones who have separated themselves from him. And we have been reflecting on how the death of Jesus on the cross has the power to bring us to a place of restoration to God.

We're going to begin today by looking at a dramatic passage in the Gospel of Matthew, chapter 27, verses 3–5:

> When Judas, his betrayer, saw that Jesus was condemned, he repented and brought back the thirty pieces of silver to the chief priests and the elders. He said, "I have sinned by betraying innocent blood." But they said, "What is that to us? See to it yourself." Throwing down the pieces of silver in the temple, he departed; and he went and hanged himself. (NRSV)

This bleak text comes just before the horror of the crucifixion descends upon Jesus. Judas—the one who responded to Jesus's call to follow him; the one who, along with the other disciples, was an answer to Jesus's prayer; the one who shared the bread and wine with him at the Last Supper—handed Jesus over to the religious leaders, who saw to it that the Romans condemned Jesus and sentenced him to death.

It appears that Judas was sorry for what he had done. Matthew says that Judas repented, that he turned away from the wrong he had done. He even confessed his sin to the religious leaders, who should have helped him: "I have sinned by betraying innocent blood." But they were no help. They gave him the worst counsel that could possibly be given: "See to it yourself." How was Judas supposed to do that? How, in his own power, could Judas fix what he had done?

He couldn't. And he knew he couldn't. He took the only route he thought was open to him: he removed himself permanently from the presence of those who were outside the apparently unforgivable offense he had committed by taking his own life.

What was it that drove Judas to such a dark and desperate place? Was it guilt? Probably not. He certainly was guilty, but even the least pious of the Jewish people knew how to deal with guilt: their law called for certain religious rituals to deal with the issue of guilt in people's lives. No, it was something that sprang out of his own guilt and took root in his heart like malignant seeds from a cancerous tumor. It was something called *shame*.

What is shame? Dr. Ray Anderson says this:

> Shame is the perceived loss of our place with others. Those who have the power to create our history have the power to make us feel worthy or unworthy at the core of our being. Since our being is dependent upon how others view us, we feel shame as loss of being. It is this deep sense of shame, which seems to deprive us of our very right to exist, that drives many over the edge of guilt to suicide.[1]

Judas saw himself as losing his place with the others who had *not* betrayed Jesus. He couldn't imagine any of the other eleven disciples doing something as hideous as he had done. He rushed to end the unbearable pain of never being able to enter back into that circle of intimacy that had lived for three years in the presence of Jesus. He didn't wait to discover that Peter had turned his back on Jesus in a cowardly way, claiming he didn't even know who Jesus was. The others just ran and hid as Jesus took the heat from the Romans. The only one of the Twelve who even came near the cross to which Jesus had been nailed was John, who accompanied the women—the only ones courageous enough to be seen publicly as Jesus's friends.

Judas never found out that his shame, while real, was not the ultimate separator he thought it had to be. The failures of his former companions did not make Judas's violation any less severe, but they did destroy the illusion that Jesus's close friends existed in a pure environment that Judas could not reenter.

When the ancient Greeks spoke of *shame*, they captured the idea of being ugly or disfigured. The words they used for shame gave a picture of someone outside of respectability, confused, and hanging his head.

Isn't that how shame impacts us? It makes a person feel like a leper, unclean, no longer allowed to stand among clean people because of one's ugliness:

Cheating in school. When you were in school, were you ever caught cheating on a test and publicly pointed out by a teacher? Suddenly you were outside the circle of clean competition. There was nothing you could do to fix it.

But what if you knew everyone else in the class was cheating as well? You might be mad that you were the only one caught, but you likely wouldn't feel any deep sense of shame. After all, you remained in "good" company.

Naked in public. One of the most common nightmares people experience is suddenly discovering themselves naked in a public place. You walk into the lobby of Edwards Theater, and everything is fine. Then you glance at the window and see your own bare reflection. And just as you realize you are naked, so does everyone else. It's like a group epiphany, with you as the focus of everyone's revelation.

Now, if you suddenly discovered that you and everyone else in the building was naked, it might be unusual and even funny, but at least you'd just blend in with the crowd.

It's easy to understand why the ancient world linked shame and nakedness together. It went all the way back to the beginning, when Adam and Eve turned away from God and suddenly became self-conscious. Their nakedness was now an issue, and they tried to disguise that fact from themselves and God by using big fig leaves (Gen. 3:7).

We have many disguises for shame:

We can deny it. It's no big deal. Or, they don't need to know. It's my business.

So we carry within us our own dark secrets, continually fooling ourselves into believing that none of it matters. But we live with the fear that, one day, someone will reveal the secret, and we will stand exposed and full of shame.

We can also run. When we believe we have disqualified ourselves from others by our actions, then we can redirect our lives so that we isolate ourselves, hoping that in our hiddenness the pain of shame won't be able to reach us.

I have to wonder about the string of high school shootings that seem to have come about because of apparent bullying. Can a young person, pushed to the edge of his own cultural world and daily shamed and humiliated, go over that edge and kill his tormentors? It seems so.

When Jesus went to the cross, God embraced human death. The death that was our consequence for carrying the guilt that comes from sin—from missing the mark, from getting off track, from wandering away from God—becomes God's death in Jesus, and in that, death loses its power.

In the death of Jesus our guilt becomes powerless in that we find forgiveness and reconciliation to God. But there's something else that must lose its power: *shame*. In the death of Jesus, our shame also dies.

How can that happen? *It happens in that Jesus shares our shame with us*. In that sharing he takes it to the cross, the place of death, and there shame loses its power over us.

Let's go back to Judas for a moment. Because of his crime, Judas saw himself as incapable of reentering Jesus's circle of acceptance. He had become an outsider. What Judas didn't wait to discover was that *Jesus himself became the ultimate outsider*:

On trial. At the initiative of his own countrymen, Jesus was bound and dragged before several kangaroo courts.

Beaten. Before being crucified, Jesus was beaten and spit upon by the Roman guards as the process of dehumanization ran its course.

Stripped. Just before being nailed to the cross, Jesus was stripped. His nakedness became part of the public spectacle of the criminal's death.

Banished. This crucifixion took place outside the city, outside of the place where normal, respectable life took place. He was banished from the world of homes, family and friends, work and play. Now he took on the identity of the condemned criminal and would forever be an *outsider*.

In the movie *Second Best* William Hurt plays a middle-aged Welsh postmaster who has been left alone in the world. His parents are dead, and he has never married. He decides he would like to adopt a child so that he can have a family. So he enters the difficult process of adoption and makes a connection with a troubled ten-year-old who sees the postmaster as a vehicle for getting him back in contact with his ex-convict father. The young boy worships his father and longs for the day when they can be together again.

The postmaster continuously reaches out to the boy, who repeatedly dismisses him. One day the boy's father unexpectedly shows up. But rather than appearing as a strong, adventurous liberator, he arrives as a broken man, ravaged by the last stages of AIDS, and unable even to care for himself. In a conflicted sense of compassion, the postmaster takes him in to die.

The young boy is torn apart by the disillusionment and shame that rolls over him, and he begins to comprehend the awful truth about both his mother and father—that they have abandoned him for their own pursuits. In this scene the boy finally takes his shame to the only place he knows to go. [*At this point the gathering viewed a video clip from the movie, showing how the story ends, as described here.*]

The boy, devastated by the image of his shattered father, runs away from the postmaster's home in the middle of the night, taking a garden shovel with him. The boy heads out into the hills, digs a hole, wraps himself up in a sleeping bag, and crawls in. The postmaster discovers the boy's absence and goes after him. When the postmaster finds him, the boy is unresponsive and will not (cannot?) move from the gravelike hole he is in. So the postmaster picks up the shovel and widens the hole, making room for himself. He then places himself in the hole, next to the boy.

In the morning, both awaken. The postmaster informs the boy that he loves him very deeply, but that the boy is free to refuse his love. But what he will not do is become the boy's "second best." In the end, as they are walking back into the village, the boy reaches up and takes the man's hand.

Some of us wonder why—even after being rescued, even after saying "yes" to God's wonderful gift of forgiveness in Jesus—we still want to crawl into a hole and die. Just dig a grave, lie down, cover up with bushes and branches and dirt, and never show our faces again. It's because while the power of guilt and sin has died, the power of shame still screams out the lie: *we continue to deserve death*. To have nothing, to be nothing, to feel nothing.

But in that hole in the ground, Jesus comes and joins us. When we have gone to the place where we thought no one would find us, we discover that Jesus has gone there with us; he has willingly embraced our shame as his own. And in the company of the ultimate outsider, we become the ultimate *insiders*. We can live inside the circle of Jesus's love, where shame can no longer be our identity.

The writer of the book of Hebrews tells us, in this journey called life, never to take our eyes off of Jesus,

> the pioneer and perfecter of our faith, who for the sake of the joy that was set before him endured the cross, disregarding its shame, and has taken his seat at the right hand of the throne of God. (12:2 NRSV)

On the cross Jesus embraces and experiences our death; in his death the power of sin to dominate us is destroyed, and eternal death is wiped out. There is no more illusion; there can be no life without God.

In his death Jesus also destroys our shame because the truth about all of us is exposed: we do not have the power to rescue ourselves. Our shame is not destroyed because we have no sin; it is destroyed because the illusion is broken that only other people have earned the right to be acceptable to God. Jesus dies a human death and dies with and for us; he dies a shameful death and destroys the power of shame to captivate, isolate, and dehumanize us.

There is an aspect of truth in our shame. It is an appropriate response to our own lives and actions as we recognize who we are before God. The falsehood is that our shame drives us outside of God's reach.

[*Hands out nails.*] I want the nails you hold in your hands today to symbolize something important, but not as symbols of our guilt, or telling us that we are the ones who hammered the nails into Jesus. Rather, hold the nail and feel its unforgiving texture and strength. Imagine these nails to be symbols of the shame that rivets itself to our souls and keeps us always the outsiders, never allowing us to see what is happening in the inner circle of God's love. Imagine that the nails of shame have been driven into you.

Now think of Jesus on the cross. Think of him going there willingly. Imagine him, as he passes by you on his way to the place of death, pulling the nails of shame out of your body, taking them with him to the cross. Those nails now have no power to exclude you from God's gigantic circle of love.

For some, this will be a reminder of the great work Jesus has already done in your life, to free you from shame's stranglehold on you. For others, this will be a time for you to have, perhaps for the first time in your life, the power of shame broken in you, so that by the power of God, the power of his Spirit, you will come away with your head lifted up. You may, today, become an insider in God's circle of love.

As you come to the table of Jesus today, bring your nail with you. Drop that nail into the bowls that are near the table. Leave your shame, and then come to the table that Jesus has set for you.

—————

At the end of the previous chapter, I offered some comments on shame and the cross and pointed to an in-depth discussion of that theme in *Recovering the Scandal of the Cross*. We will not further explore that theme here. I would, however, like to highlight the way that McNichols has used nails, but in a way different from how speakers commonly use them in presentations on penal satisfaction. I applaud the way McNichols has done this because it illustrates the possibility of reinterpreting rather than discarding symbols of penal satisfaction.

McNichols ends his sermon with an invitation meaningful for Christians, as well as evangelistic for non-Christians. In fact, a woman who had been an angry, dedicated anti-Christian atheist responded positively to this invitation, placed her trust in Jesus, and became part of this community of faith.

15

A Father's Advocacy

Ryan Schellenberg

Like Mike McNichols in the previous chapter, Ryan Schellenberg focuses on the theme of shame as he proclaims the saving significance of Jesus's life, death, and resurrection in a North American context. As he developed this metaphorical narrative, Schellenberg had in mind those who have experienced the watchful eye of a close-knit conservative evangelical community. He gave this presentation to fellow seminary students in April 2005 at Mennonite Brethren Biblical Seminary in Fresno, California.

I grew up the son of a pastor—a hazardous occupation at the best of times, and even more like walking through a minefield when your father's church is located in a small, isolated, rural, and conservative community. Thanks in part to Paul's offhanded comment that someone who can't keep his own kids in line probably can't effectively parent a church (1 Tim. 3:4–5), and in part to the notorious predilection of small-town folk for talking about scandal, my father's reputation and effectiveness in ministry were intimately correlated with the quiet decency of my behavior. I soon learned that jumping from gravestone to gravestone in the church cemetery after a Sunday service was not permissible, and that although it was okay to shuffle my feet on the carpet of the sanctuary, it was incumbent upon me to find victimless ways of discharging the buildup of static electricity. Being a pastor's son is a difficult job for anyone, and particularly for a ten-year-old boy with an innate propensity for mischief.

One Sunday afternoon, before I was well acquainted with my job description, my family hosted an elderly and well-respected church member for dinner. I don't recall his name, but I'll call him Abe Reimer—and considering the narrow spectrum of names current in our Mennonite Brethren community, the odds are quite good that I've guessed at least his first or last name correctly. Abe Reimer, I was later to learn, was saddened by my father's introduction of the New International Version into our Sunday services. But he was a reasonable man. Unlike Victor Enns, who was too strident about his convictions to gain much of a hearing in the church, Mr. Reimer did not think the King James Version was the only real Bible. He just preferred the familiar and lyrical words with which he had walked through life. Our community valued and respected his humbly articulated beliefs.

On this particular Sunday, I was at the top of my form. After dinner, instead of running outside to join my brother in a game of soccer—which my parents certainly permitted on the Sabbath but which I feared might offend Mr. Reimer—I retired with the men to our living room for some edifying conversation. I listened respectfully, I didn't interrupt, and I answered Mr. Reimer's polite inquiries with utmost sincerity. But somewhere along the way my sincerity betrayed me.

"What do you keep yourself busy with, Ryan?" he asked.

"I like to listen to music," I replied. I suspected that music was a more appropriate topic for a Sunday afternoon than the fort I had built in the nearby brush.

"And what kind of music do you enjoy?"

"I really like Steve Taylor," I offered, naively imagining that our household favorite was equally appreciated by our neighbors.

"I'm not familiar with Steve Taylor," Mr. Reimer admitted. "What kind of music does he sing?"

"Oh, it's great!" I explained. "He sings Christian rock music."

Mr. Reimer's brow furrowed, and his glance shifted from me to my father—though he replied in the same slightly condescending tone he had used while addressing me.

"Ryan, there is no such thing as *Christian* rock music."

Confused, I too turned to look at my father, who sat silently for a moment, solemnly watching me. By the time my father spoke, I had managed to decipher the nonverbal darts flying across the room. I had somehow made a dreadful mistake. I had obviously offended Mr. Reimer and had clearly put my father in an awkward position. I blushed ashamedly, sank back into the sofa, and tried to disappear.

But though I had read the cues well enough to be ashamed, I was angry too. I couldn't understand what I had done wrong. After all, it was my father who had bought the Steve Taylor tape. He liked Christian rock music too. I was sure he did. This just wasn't fair.

After a moment, my dad turned back to Mr. Reimer. His eyes had become animated, and his face took on the intensity it did when he was preaching or telling Bible stories.

"Well, Abe, I'm not sure about that," my dad replied softly. "I think some of those musicians are writing wonderful songs."

As I relaxed and the fire in my cheeks subsided, my dad got out the lyrics to Steve Taylor's newest record and read Mr. Reimer the words of one of my favorite songs. It was called "Whatever Happened to Sin," and my father explained that it was an attempt to counter our society's easy tolerance of moral relativism. Though I didn't understand the conversation at all, I knew I belonged in that room, on the sofa beside my father, privy to the discussion of the men.

The repercussions of my father's advocacy were not disastrous. After all, Mr. Reimer was a reasonable man. I doubt that he left our home a new fan of the genre, but he didn't leave an enemy either. My father remained a well-liked and appreciated pastor, and his fondness for Christian rock music was quietly forgotten.

Luke's story of the ministry of Jesus is surprisingly similar to the story of that Sunday afternoon, though Jesus doesn't get off the hook quite as easily as my father did. Throughout his Gospel, Luke shows Jesus advocating on behalf of those considered sinners by the religious establishment. Let's drop in for a moment on Luke's tale:

> One sabbath while Jesus was going through the grainfields, his disciples plucked some heads of grain, rubbed them in their hands, and ate them. But some of the Pharisees said, "Why are you doing what is not lawful on the sabbath?" (6:1–2 NRSV)

Think of how Jesus's disciples must have felt. This is a motley handful of Galilean fishermen. They aren't prepared for legal debates with these intimidating and respected elders. The Pharisees know the law; the disciples can't argue. They can do nothing but hang their heads in shame. They're like ten-year-old boys caught listening to rock music on a Sunday afternoon. But look how Jesus responds:

> "Have you not read what David did when he and his companions were hungry? He entered the house of God and took and ate the bread of the Presence, which it is not lawful for any but the priests to eat, and gave some to his companions?" Then he said to them, "The Son of Man is lord of the sabbath." (vv. 3–5 NRSV)

Notice carefully what Jesus does here: he makes himself and his disciples the equals of the legendary King David and his band of mighty men. Jesus defends the dignity of his followers against the accusation of the religious elite by putting his own identity on the line. No longer a ragtag bunch of hicks, Jesus's disciples are honored companions of David's awaited heir. They are under the protection of God's anointed one.

Luke's story of Jesus is filled with such encounters. The lowly, broken people of Israel—those routinely put to shame by the pious Pharisees—are given new dignity as Jesus provides them with a new sense of belonging. Notorious sinners become Jesus's guests of honor (7:36–50). The "unclean" too are sons and daughters of Abraham (13:16; 19:9); these too belong to the people of God.

But by gathering those of questionable piety into a new community of belonging, Jesus incurs the indignation of the religious. Like my father, who put his reputation on the line to protect my dignity, Jesus risks his own neck to defend the honor of all God's children. Unfortunately, the elders of Israel weren't as charitable as Abe Reimer was. The influential and respected leaders of the religious community were deeply offended and demanded Jesus's resignation. When his resignation was not forthcoming, Jesus was fired and publicly humiliated. Yes, that cross—that "emblem of suffering and shame"—was the accusers' response to Jesus's advocacy on behalf of God's lost children.

Imagine another end to the story of my Sunday afternoon in rural Saskatchewan. Imagine a guest more like the Pharisees, who after hearing my father's response lashes out in indignant condemnation of Steve Taylor and all who hear his abominable music. And imagine my father, refusing to concede the point, but also unwilling to lash back—unwilling to speak words that threaten his guest's dignity. Surely I would have wondered, as Jesus's disciples must have on that dark Friday night, whose verdict really mattered. Is my father wrong? Is he too weak to guard his honor—and mine—by decisively proving his point? Why doesn't he stand up for us?

And now for a real leap of the imagination: Can you visualize our guest's surprise if, after three minutes of my agonizing shame, the psalmist King David himself walks into the room and quietly expresses his respect for Steve Taylor's songwriting? (I know it sounds ridiculous, but is it any more incredible than resurrection?) And can you imagine my delight and my burgeoning pride? I keep rather good company after all, don't I? I may be just a ten-year-old boy, but I belong in this conversation. I have a place here.

That wasn't the last time my father stood up for me, and I wasn't always innocent of wrongdoing when he did so. But that day did mark a turning point in my career as a pastor's son. As the son of my father, I sought to behave with dignity to match how he treated me. But I didn't need to defend my father's honor; he was defending mine! Even when I made it rather awkward for him, he wasn't about to let me be put to shame. After all, I was his son.

In the previous chapter McNichols's presentation climaxes at the cross; here Schellenberg's pivotal moment is the resurrection. Yet, like a number of others in this book, Schellenberg portrays Jesus's life, death, and resurrection as a coherent whole—three intimately related moments in a single event.

The presentation focuses on how God provides salvation from shame through affirming our dignity as God's children. I appreciate, however, that Schellenberg also includes the reality that we are saved for something. He points toward the biblical emphasis on actualizing our newly affirmed identity as children of God through appropriate behavior.

Commenting on the presentation to other students, Schellenberg noted:

> The story dissolves the tension between objective and subjective theories of the atonement. The objective event is not a change in quasi-legal status but is rather a real and concrete transformation of the social reality—a transformation that the protagonist experiences and responds to through a new (subjective) understanding of his personal and social identity. Accordingly, salvation is both a personal/spiritual and a social/relational reality.

Another comment from Schellenberg also relates to themes I discussed in the introductory chapter of this book and in our previous book: "The revelation of God's character in this metaphor is almost an exact inversion of the image of God posited by Anselm's model: the cross isn't about satisfying God's honor; the cross reveals God's willingness to risk his honor in order to guard ours."

The concreteness of the ten-year-old boy's experience of shame allows many to connect with the story, even those outside the conservative evangelical subculture. The reality, however, is that the narrative is much more effective within that subculture. That, however, is more observation than critique. Schellenberg's presentation fulfills well the ideal of contextualization. It presents the gospel in a way that both connects with and challenges a particular context. The story communicates the meaning of the atonement in images taken from the concrete and everyday experiences of conservative evangelicalism, but it tries to challenge the religiosity upon which that subculture is built.

In relation to this challenge, I want to applaud and highlight two aspects in the story. First, although Abe Reimer is pharisaically religious in the story, Schellenberg nuances the character. This can serve to remind us that the Pharisees were more complex than how we often caricature them, and that, like Mr. Reimer and Mr. Enns, individual Pharisees certainly also brought a variety of motivations and degrees of severity to their practice of religious judgmentalism. Closer to home, Schellenberg's portrayal of Abe Reimer nudges us to recognize something of ourselves in Mr. Reimer, rather than simply putting ourselves in the "non-Pharisee" category because we do not draw lines of religious judgmentalism with the severity that Victor Enns does.

Second, although the sin of the ten-year-old was not the focus of the story, he was not quite innocent. His somewhat duplicitous attempts to impress Mr. Reimer signal his choice to enter the web of religiosity and status-maintenance that quickly becomes the means of his downfall. Both Schellenberg's living-room narrative and the compared Lukan narrative do portray a clear sense of a victim and a victimizer. Nevertheless, this hint of the boy's status seeking through religiosity reminds the listener that the line of distinction between human victim and victimizer is blurry and runs through each of our hearts.

Present

Luci Shaw

In *Recovering the Scandal of the Cross*, we sought to make a contribution to the biblical, theological, and missiological discussion about the atonement. This book seeks to contribute alternative images for our presentations of the atonement. We need new stories; we also need new poems and songs. Although some poems, choruses, and hymns do explicitly portray a penal satisfaction understanding of the atonement, many others do not. Unfortunately, many people interpret most all poetic imagery of the cross in penal categories since they view it through the lenses of penal satisfaction. Therefore, in worship leading we must explicitly call people's attention to nonpenal imagery and encourage the writing of poetic imagery like that in Luci Shaw's poem, which clearly broadens the meaning of the cross and includes the resurrection as part of God's atoning work.[1] Following the poem, Shaw provides a commentary on its context.

Present
(with thanks to Tony Campolo)

At light-speed, God-speed,
time collapses into *now* so that

we may see Christ's wounds as
still bleeding, his torso,
that ready sponge, still
absorbing our vice, our toxic shame.

He is still being pierced
by every hateful nail
we hammer home. In this
Golgotha moment his body—
chalice for the dark tears
of the whole world—brims,

spilling over as his lifeblood
drains. His dying into the earth
begins the great reversal—
as blood from a vein leaps
into the needle, so with his rising,
we surge into light.

I'd been having some blood tests. Since I am not needle-pho-
bic, I am always fascinated to watch the way the arterial blood
pulses its way through the needle inserted into the fat vein in
the crook of my arm. I *like* to look. The technician first circles
my arm with an elastic tourniquet, taps at that underlying vein
to make it pop up, then pokes in the sharp needle ("Just a little
prick now . . ."). The red fluid seems eager to move through the
needle in quick bursts into the technician's syringe, to be labeled,
sealed, and sent to the lab for analysis.

Shortly after such a blood test I was at a fund-raising dinner for
an international Christian mission organization. Tony Campolo
was the speaker, and in the context of his message he emphasized
how God's time is not restricted to our linear concepts of past,
present, and future. God is outside of time, so that for him all of
reality is always present. It is all happening *now*. That meant that
Jesus' death on the cross is present for me, in all its horror and
beauty. The interaction of his death and its result in my atonement
is an ongoing relationship. The sins I may daily commit may be
daily expunged in his daily dying. His resurrection and mine, as
part of his body, is also a present and welcome reality.

This is such a powerful notion. I felt transfixed by its potential,
and in further conversation with Campolo (I was at his table),

we enlarged the idea. On the plane homeward, I wrote the poem above and later sent it to Campolo, who then circulated it in his newsletter. The idea of the huge reversal, from the downward trajectory of human failure and death to the upward surge into forgiveness and life and light, is still so potently authentic for me. In memory I visualize the rhythmic movement of the bright blood leaping from the vein, reminding me how Jesus leaped from the tomb.

17

Salvation through the Sacrifice of God's Firstborn Son

Gwinyai H. Muzorewa

The following is a Good Friday sermon preached in a United Methodist Church in Zimbabwe, to Christians from the Shona tribe. Although set in an urban context, those congregated had strong ties to their rural past and would identify a rural town or village as "home."

"Blood sacrifice" is a foreign concept for many people in the world today, yet for many others, such as the Shona in Africa, blood sacrifices and rituals involving blood are part of life, or at least within memory. For such persons, biblical sacrificial language communicates powerfully the saving significance of the cross and resurrection.

When viewed through the lens of penal satisfaction, biblical sacrifices become payments made to appease God. Although some African cultures do understand some sacrifices as payments, more commonly in Africa the role of a sacrifice is to cleanse, to break a barrier or curse, or to seal a covenant.[1] Looking through the lens of African culture can lead us to a different understanding of the sacrificial language in the

Bible. In this sermon, Gwinyai Muzorewa uses metaphors from the Shona culture, the firstborn son and blood sacrifice, to provide alternatives to the penal satisfaction understanding of the atonement, which Christians from the North brought to Africans.

Bishop Christopher Jokomo introduced the Rev. Dr. Gwinyai Muzorewa to the congregation and then said:

> Dr. Muzorewa, here is one of our many mushrooming congregations in Zimbabwe. God has called you to preach on this Good Friday the "good news" that Jesus Christ died an excruciating and yet sacrificial and salvific death on the cross in order that our sins may be forgiven. God gave his own Son as a ransom for many, . . . indeed, for all. Did God really subject his Son to this kind of death, just to please God's self? Just what is the meaning of the atonement? How do you understand this core message of our faith? How is it that this death pleased God? How is it that the suffering of an innocent person should be used to "free" the sinful world? Is it really salvific? Assuming that Jesus is God, according to trinitarian theology, why would God [meaning Jesus Christ] pay God for our sins?

Then Dr. Muzorewa rose from his chair and went to the podium to preach:

Thank you, Bishop Jokomo.

Let us pray: Eternal God, Eternal Son, and the Eternal Holy Spirit, this morning I pray for the spiritual enlightenment that comes only from you, as I begin to share the good news that it pleased you to give up your only begotten Son for a salvific purpose. Oh, may we be forever grateful to you; give us the spirit of celebration, rather than mourning; the spirit of victory, rather than death; the spirit of delight, rather than sadness. Amen.

My sermon topic this morning is, "When bad news is good news." The substance of my sermon is the meaning of the atonement. Over the years my soul has evolved from thinking of Easter as *bad news*, to regarding the death, resurrection, and ascension as *good news*. Today I invite you to revisit that saga with me. Needless to say, this has to be a prayerful spiritual journey. When we celebrate the Easter event, we thank God for what God has done through the Son Jesus Christ. He suffered and died on the cross, was buried, and on the third day God raised him from the dead so that we may have life and have it abundantly. Today, on this Good Friday, nothing is more appropriate than to reflect on why we talk about Good Friday when at the same time we are remembering the suffering and death of our Lord Jesus Christ.

FIRSTBORN SON

Jesus is God's firstborn Son. We always recite this in the [Nicene] Creed: "God gave his *only* begotten Son." I am sure that those of us who have families realize the magnitude of this statement. In our families we know that we expect much of the firstborn son. He is a blessing to the family's posterity. He will carry the family name. And in carrying the name, the implication is that the father, though he die, yet will he live, *through the son*. In this sense, the son, the firstborn son, is his father's pleasure. He may often assume his responsibilities even while his father is still alive. The whole family tends to look up to this special family member. And the firstborn son enjoys *being* what he is, and so he *willingly* does all that is expected of him.

Although the firstborn son never would expect his father or his family to "punish" him, or to trade him off for pleasure, he knows that if they need someone to expiate, or break, a "curse" on the family, he would have to be the one because he carries the name of the clan or family. The firstborn is prepared to sacrifice for the sake of his family's spiritual and physical well-being. He is cognizant of the fact that he will receive blessings and yet also shoulder curses on behalf of his family. A responsible firstborn son will rather die than watch his father perish before his face.

The firstborn son is certainly the beloved child of the father. Indeed, there is a kind of mutual interdependence between father and son. True, the rest of the children are loved, but the firstborn son is *most beloved*. Put bluntly, he holds a position that comes with glorious benefits and rewards, but also *with great respon-sibilities*. Does not our culture target certain responsibilities for the firstborn son? Who must be first to do the will of his father?

We answer, "The firstborn son." There may be variations from one ethnic group to the next, but the principle still stands.

For instance, among us here, the Shona of Zimbabwe, the firstborn plays the *priestly* role when the occasion arises to make a sacrifice to the ancestors. Or, when a daughter is getting married, the firstborn son plays the role of *Baba* [father]. He is in charge of collecting the *lobola* [bridal price]. He stands in place of his father when there is a court hearing in the village and the father is unable to attend.

The firstborn son is indeed, as we say, the *right-hand man* of the father. Only he can perform many rituals if they are to be efficacious. For instance, when a big banquet is planned during the rainy season, on a day it might rain, the firstborn is asked to perform a certain ritual that would keep rains from falling for the rest of the day until the banquet is over! (The big Auntie heats a hoe until it is red-hot, and the firstborn digs just once in the earth near the house, using this hoe, and leaves it in that position for the rest of the day. It will not rain!) In our own family, my brother performs this and other rituals. Anyone else who performed a ritual designated for the firstborn son would commit a taboo. This morning I can tell you that *mukoma* [title for boy's older brother] Tendakai Muzorewa enjoys his role as not only the eldest child but also as the firstborn son. He will do anything for the family and for the sake of the family's name.

The birth of the firstborn has great significance. This child is the first "fruit of the marriage" between husband and wife. In our culture, we say, he is the one who "opens the mother's womb." This symbolizes perfection, being a blessing, one who represents all. He is the first, tangible symbol of God's blessing for this marriage. He is God's sign for consent and approval of this relationship. He is the covenant child, a child of God's promise and agreement. He stands between heaven and earth for the particular family.

JESUS AS *MUKOMA*: VICARIOUS SERVICE TO THE FAMILY

Now that we have thought about how precious the firstborn son is in our families, let me share with you how special and precious God's firstborn Son, Jesus Christ, is. He is *mukoma* par excellence. According to the Scriptures, he is the firstborn of heaven (Heb. 1:1–6). By virtue of his position in God's family, the *Christian family*, only *he* can perform certain family *chores and rituals*.

Let us think specifically about the meaning of Good Friday in relation to Jesus as the firstborn Son of God. His mind-set is like that of the firstborn son of any of our families. His joy is to serve to the fullest in his capacity. For this reason Jesus once said to his disciples: "My food is to do the will of him who sent me and to finish his work" (John 4:34 NRSV). Put differently, for Jesus, life was meaningful only if he did the will of his Father. The abundant life he came to give us was part of his commitment to doing the will of his Father. Now, brothers and sisters, if Jesus's will was to be inseparable from his Father, if Jesus found satisfaction from pleasing his Father, and if Jesus as the Son and God as the Father were *one*—then we are to understand Good Friday as the point of consummation.

The crucifixion was a moment of atonement, or restoration of our relationships with God. The cross was a special event, a spiritual rendezvous where God and humanity, alienated by sin, came together in Jesus's humanity, which was without blemish. For the sake of our salvation, sin was expiated, or "taken away." When Christ walked on earth, it pleased God that he healed the sick, cured the lame, gave sight to the blind, and even raised the dead. Similarly, the expiation of our sin pleases God, who hates sin. Good Friday is *good news* because through the removal of sin, humanity is "made good," sanctified, and justified. In addition, the resurrection of Jesus Christ, which is inextricably related to the crucifixion and death, brings more good news because it symbolizes immortality.

Of the various forms of vicarious atonement, the Christian atonement has a peculiar dimension to it in that in his true humanity and true divinity, Jesus is clearly the only *one* who "taketh away . . . the sins of the whole world" (John 1:29 and 1 John 2:2 KJV). This is so for several reasons:

1. Jesus is a true human being, whose blood was shed in the presence of God and at God's pleasure in order that the sacrifice is efficacious. What pleased God is not the death but the *atonement*; Jesus's death was not punishment by

God or payment to God for the sins of the whole world. Rather, it was the saving act that only the firstborn Son could perform efficaciously. Thus, it was the Son's pleasure to save everybody in the family. It was an act of self-actualization. It was accomplishment, rather than punishment imposed on him by his father.

2. Jesus was without sin. He was a "lamb without blemish," a quality necessary for the sacrificial lamb. It had to be Jesus's pleasure to be the only one capable of what no other creation or divinity could do. What pleased God, then, was not the death, but the willingness to do good for goodness' sake.

3. Jesus's will and that of his Father were mutual. He himself repeatedly said, "My Father and I are one" (John 10:30 NRSV); neither the Son nor the Father could please the other outside of one's own pleasure.

4. In his two natures, Jesus was both the "priest" and the "sacrificial lamb," as well as the one to receive the sacrifice in his capacity as God.

Did Jesus die when he willingly took up the cross and proceeded from this life through death to resume eternal living? We believe he did so willingly, and the creeds testify that he bled and died on the cross. Such sanguineous dying was a clear form of sacrifice. Understood as self-giving, sacrificial death served the purpose of "making right" the sins of the whole world. The bleeding on the cross is similar to the self-giving suffering that *mukoma* endures when he goes through the various rites of passage designated for the firstborn son. The "old boy" dies, to be replaced by the "new man" emerging from the rites of passage. Actually, the gushing blood is a necessary symbol in the dying process. Courage and commitment are measured by letting one's blood flow while the victim focuses his attention on that for which the blood is spilled. Not only is there a feeling of victory but also a sense of efficacy in that moment of consciousness.

The point of the rites of passage is to transform the individual from being a "boy or child" to being "a man or young adult." In that process, there is joy over the young man's triumphant metamorphosis. We do not think of the rites of passage as some form of punishment, or some form of payment so that he can become an adult. Nor is the entire process an imposition on the young man. To the contrary, it is something he has looked forward to, although not in a sadomasochistic way.

In the case of Jesus, he says about his own life: "No one takes it from me, but I lay it down of my own accord. I have authority to lay it down and authority to take it up again" (John 10:18 NIV). There is that total willingness to die a sacrificial death in order to save all creation, because in his dying all shall live. This deed, I believe, is what pleased the Father. Jesus's death is a gracious expression of God's love, which results in the salvation of all creation (John 3:16–17; Rom. 8:21–23). Furthermore, as it pleases the African father to see his son go through the suffering to manhood, so it pleased God the Father that Christ "drank the cup." In the Jewish tradition, drinking the cup is willingly accepting an undertaking with all its consequences (Mark 10:38–39; 14:36).

In relation to the question of who should pay the price of our sin, think of our culture's ritual of healing. Not just anyone is allowed to donate the sacrificial beast. The actual patient may not donate the beast to be sacrificed, no matter how many the ill one has available and suitable for the purpose. The logic is that the father must donate the animal in order to show that he cares. It is the desire of the parent to have health restored to his child, whom an enemy might have harmed. Proper protocol must be observed because everything contributes to the efficaciousness of the ritual. The sacrificial victim itself must be willing to "go through" the ritual. An unwilling sacrificial animal does not make a successful offering. By comparison, God the Father did not coerce God the Son to "drink the cup." Christ and the Father are of one accord: "My Father and I are one."

As God's only begotten Son, the firstborn of heaven, Jesus was the only individual whose blood would be efficacious enough to expiate the sins of the whole world. We must understand that Jesus is God, and God is the Lord of all creation, which stood in need of salvation. Just any Jew would not suffice, just any African would not suffice, just any European or American Caucasian would not suffice. It had to be One who is "all in all." The atonement called for one who is fully human and fully divine at once.

One more point of observation. The beast "without blemish" that is chosen for the sacrifice must have a certain spirituality about it that separates it, or sets it apart, from the rest of the livestock. Similarly, Jesus was not just one more man walking the face of the earth. He has always been the Son of God. He is God incarnate, born of the Virgin Mary.

This presentation of the atonement in a Shona context by Gwinyai Muzorewa is important for several reasons, three of which bear mentioning here. The first relates to how this sermon contributes to our understanding of substitutionary atonement; the second and third relate to the challenge of articulating the message of the atonement.

Many find it difficult to conceive of substitutionary atonement, or Jesus's death as a sacrifice, in any way other than as a penal sacrificial offering of payment or appeasement. Muzorewa clearly displays how the Shona understand sacrifices, including substitutionary sacrifices, as working in ways other than appeasement. Sacrifices may break a curse, for instance. Obviously, the fact that the Shona have this understanding of blood sacrifices does not prove that Hebrew culture shared this same view. It does, however, underscore the reality that there are various uses of blood sacrifices, and that people do understand many to work in ways other than paying a penalty. Taking off a set of lenses influenced by a punishment-oriented legal system and putting on a set of Shona lenses leads to a different reading of biblical texts on sacrifice. Muzorewa's examples do not, by themselves, instruct us in the biblical understandings of sacrifices, but they can help us see aspects of the biblical sacrifices that have been hidden or distorted by the lenses many of us wear.

At the level of proclamation, I expect that readers whose contexts still have a tradition or memory of blood sacrifice will find Muzorewa's presentation especially helpful. Those of us from contexts without a current tradition of blood sacrifice may find the examples Muzorewa uses interesting, even enlightening, but such images may not connect in the depths of our being. We might have a certain intellectual grasp of the efficacy of sacrificial death and yet be left with questions: How does this work? How does the son's death help the rest of the family, or how does the animal's shed blood heal?

Even for those of us from cultures that do not practice blood sacrifice, though, Muzorewa's sermon offers two important lessons. First, it puts us in the place of trying to understand the meaning of the atonement through metaphors foreign to us. That is not ideal. We would do well to recognize that others may experience our metaphors as foreign too.[2] Second, what Muzorewa has done, we all need to do. He uses traditions, experiences, and practices from the Shona cultural context to explain to the Shona the saving significance of the cross.

18

He Shared Our Aches

Curtis Chang

Recovering the Scandal of the Cross contains excerpts from a presentation on the cross that Curtis Chang gave to an audience of university students. I appreciated the contextuality, creativity, and theological depth of the narrative and participatory drama he used.[1] I hoped that Chang could provide the script of another dramatic presentation of the atonement for this book. Although he did not have one in finished form, he did send a sermon that I am pleased to include in this book.

Chang has been the teaching pastor at the River Church Community since 2001. The church began in 1997 as a congregation of highly educated professionals located in one of the wealthiest neighborhoods of the Silicon Valley. In 2002 the senior leadership team led the church to relocate in the much more socially and economically diverse neighborhood of downtown San Jose. That costly move grew out of theological reflection that the gospel spoke about God's concern for this world (and not just the world to come) and a conviction that God has a special concern for the spiritually and socially marginalized of this world. An important task of a teacher at the River Church, then, is to help people understand the actual impact of the cross, especially for those who are most hurting in this world.

Chang preached this sermon on December 4, 2004. Although as readers you cannot see the opening video clip or PowerPoint slides, I have included notes in the text to report what the audience was seeing.

———

Opening: video clip of *One True Thing* (a doctor delivering his diagnosis of cancer to a family during the Christmas season).

INTRODUCTION

Some of you might be wondering, "Why in the world did they show such a depressing clip?" Culturally, we've come to expect Christmas to involve cheerful feelings about family, food, and presents, not a doctor pronouncing such a serious diagnosis. But if you strip aside our cultural meanings of Christmas and get back to the biblical meaning of the original event, this scene is actually quite appropriate. Christmas is God's response to an extremely serious condition that afflicts humanity.

This is why when asked to explain his purpose, Jesus gave this reply:

> *Slide*: Jesus answered, "Those who are well have no need of a physician, but those who are sick." (Luke 5:31 NRSV)

By taking on the role of the physician for a sick humanity, Jesus embodied a characteristic of God that was well-established in the Old Testament.

> *Same slide*: He heals the brokenhearted,
> and binds up their wounds. (Ps. 147:3 NRSV)

THE HUMAN CONDITION: CHRONIC ALIENATION

If Jesus arrived as a physician for humanity's sickness, the natural question is, "What is the sickness?" What is the nature of our wounds that he came to heal? According to the Bible, humanity suffers from the chronic condition of sin.

Slide: Diagnosis: Chronic Condition of Sin (or Alienation)

The essence of sin is this condition of alienation, especially alienation from God. Sin is separation, a splitting of what should be joined. It's important to understand sin not just as wrongful actions, but more deeply as a wrongful condition. Sin is the state of separation and alienation, especially from God. We certainly all have in various ways chosen actions that alienate us from God. None of us are morally innocent. But even those specific sinful actions are just symptoms of the deeper condition of alienation.

And that condition of being separated or alienated from God has been chronic to humanity. Genesis, chapter 3, tells the story of the prototypical human beings, Adam and Eve. The story conveys how this alienation infected humanity from almost the beginning. The chapter describes how alienation begins with our alienation from God, but then like a virus, it multiplies and spreads to every level of human existence. We all experience symptoms of this alienated condition.

Slide: Diagnosis: Chronic Sin (or Alienation)
    Symptom 1: Alienation from God (Gen. 3:8)
    Symptom 2: Alienation from each other (3:12)
    Symptom 3: Alienation from our own bodies (3:16, 19)
    Symptom 4: Alienation from creation and work (3:17–19)

RECOGNIZING THE SYMPTOMS

Do you recognize any of these symptoms of sin in your life? For instance, are you experiencing alienation from God? Perhaps it is an issue of obedience to God that keeps separating you from enjoying his presence. But it could also be that you find yourself stuck in a period of prayerlessness and disconnection from God that can't be explained by any active disobedience on your part. That happens. It happens to me. It's part of the human condition.

People in our community are certainly well acquainted with symptom 2. Many of us have experienced alienation in our relationships: divorce, broken friendships, breakdowns between parents and children. Broader social forces also separate us from each other. As a church, we moved here to downtown San Jose in order to try to overcome the barriers between the haves and have-nots of society. If you participate in some of our concrete attempts to bridge the gap—such as our overseas projects or our upcoming Christmas dinner for the homeless—you will experience firsthand the many things that keep us from fully relating with one another.

The have-nots especially suffer from alienation in work. Someone who couldn't attend college has much greater difficulty in joining the workforce. And the available jobs tend to be quite alienating. People do not usually wholeheartedly embrace flipping hamburgers or cleaning stalls. Even if you have a higher paying job, you can still suffer from lack of engagement, with no deep interest in the work and its purpose.

Sin as a Virus

I am familiar with all of these different expressions of sin. But I consider myself something of an expert on what I've listed here as symptom 3. I've suffered from a number of chronic physical ailments. One of my more serious ones is chronic hepatitis.

This disease bears some of the hallmarks of how sin as a condition operates in the world. Like I said, sin is more a human condition than just a specific moral action. I suffer from hepatitis not because I did something wrong, but because I was born into a wrong condition. My mother passed the disease on to me in the birth process, and she likely received it from her mother. Because of its infectious nature, hepatitis is endemic to certain populations in East Asia as it spreads from one generation to the next.

The infectiousness of sin is why some in the Christian tradition use the term "original sin." We use this term in trying to capture the endemic quality of sin that is inescapable for someone born into the human condition.

My hepatitis also bears another trait of sin in that it is quite resistant to treatment. I take medication that helps to curb the disease, but it doesn't rid my body of the virus. The hepatitis virus, like many viruses such as HIV, is quite sneaky in mutating and getting around each new drug, so I have had to take multiple drugs just to keep the disease under control.

These drugs are analogous to how the Bible views laws that govern behavior (even God-given laws found in Scripture). Obeying laws and practicing generally good moral behavior can help control sin from growing rampantly. But they do not heal the underlying condition of sin. And in fact, sin has a way of ultimately evading any attempt at behavioral control.

Finally, the actual way the virus does its damage is terribly consistent with the nature of sin as alienation. The hepatitis virus, like most viruses, deceives the body into making war against itself, causing my immune system to attack otherwise healthy liver cells. My body is literally alienated from itself.

And there is no true cure out there. It's a chronic condition. Those of you who also suffer from chronic conditions know how on our worst days we can descend into a hopelessness about the future. That's the nature of chronic conditions. It tells you, "It's just always going to be this bad. No one can heal you." You feel like you're in it alone.

This hopelessness is yet another symptom of alienation. It is the feeling that no one else really can help or even understand. This is why in Jeremiah 30, God diagnoses Israel's sinful condition by using the language of chronic disease and alienation.

> *Slide*: For thus says the LORD: Your hurt is incurable, your wound is grievous. There is no one to uphold your cause, no medicine for your wound, no healing for you. All your [friends] . . . have forgotten you; they care nothing for you. (12–14 NRSV)

WHO WILL CHOOSE US?

For myself, the alienating nature of my condition led me in my early twenties to question whether I would ever get married. Who, after all, would want to expose themselves to my condition? My doubt was only partially about the risk of infection that a potential spouse would have to face (there was at the time a newly developed vaccine for hepatitis that would significantly reduce that risk for a potential spouse). My greater doubt surrounded other forms of risk and exposure. Whoever married me would be marrying someone with a far greater chance of serious health breakdown. Who wants to expose themselves to the possibility that they will have to nurse a chronically ill person? I'm also at a far greater risk for liver cancer and a number of other potentially fatal ailments. Someone who started a family with me would be exposing themselves to the risk of becoming a widow. Why would someone take that chance? And so I seriously wondered whether I would ever get married.

Even with all these questions, I somehow still found myself getting into a relationship with a woman named Jody. I certainly made no secret about my various health issues (especially my other main chronic health condition, severe back pain). But in the early blushes of a romance—especially with somebody as fun, beautiful, and enjoyable as she was—I found myself concentrating on things other than viruses and statistics of risk probabilities. When we started getting more serious and talking about marriage, however, I began to wonder whether Jody really knew the risk she was facing.

So I sat down with her and tried to lay it out as clearly as I could. Actually, I think I was being especially alarmist, talking about her becoming a single mother and other scenarios. Maybe I was unconsciously testing whether she could be scared away. I concluded by asking, "Do you really know what you're getting into here?" She paused and was quite thoughtful for a while. Then she replied, "I know that. I'm choosing that. I'm choosing you."

THE INCARNATION

What would an answer to alienation sound like? What would be the first sign that a cure might actually exist?

It would be the sound and sights of the first Christmas. When Jesus the infant cried out in birth, when the sight of his body first emerged, that was God saying, "I know this. I'm choosing this. I'm choosing you." Christmas is the celebration of the incarnation: God coming in the form of Jesus and choosing to share fully in the human condition. In the incarnation, God has chosen you, and me, and all of humanity.

Jesus chose to fully share our condition, including our condition of sin. He chose a full and complete exposure. We often don't realize how deeply Jesus shared our sin with us. Partly this is because Jesus did not commit any sinful actions. In that sense, he was perfectly innocent of sin in terms of choices or behavior. Yet somehow, without sharing in sinful actions, he took our sin, our alienation into his very being.

> *Slide*: For our sake [God] . . . made him to be sin who knew no sin, so that in him we might become the righteousness of God. (2 Cor. 5:21 NRSV)

Only Jesus could risk sharing our condition because only Jesus could overcome the condition. Only Jesus could share our alienated condition within himself and actually make it right, so that in him we might become, as the verse says, "the righteousness of God." Why? Because he is the only one who is both fully God and fully human in one united person. That's what the incarnation means: in one person God and humanity were united in Jesus.

Think of it this way. Imagine that a deadly virus is spreading across the world. It's like a strain of AIDS or the Ebola virus, a disease that rips apart its victims mercilessly. The virus replicates rapidly, kills everyone it infects, and defies any treatment.

Finally, one person steps forward and volunteers to ingest the virus. He volunteers to get among the dying victims. He allows himself to be breathed upon, spat upon, and held. He will even open up a vein and bleed with the victims. He does this because he claims that he alone can withstand this strain of the virus. By being infected but without succumbing to the disease, he claims his body can produce the antibodies that give resistance to this virus. He plans then to donate his body and blood to everyone else, so that all may acquire the same resistance.

Only the person of Jesus could risk such a choice. Only the Incarnate One could ingest the virus of alienation that would separate every other human from God, and yet not succumb to the disease. Because only Jesus is the Incarnate One: the unique and perfect union of God and humanity.

> *Slide*: For God has done what the law, weakened by the flesh, could not do: by sending his own Son in the likeness of

sinful flesh, and to deal with sin, he condemned sin in the flesh. (Rom. 8:3 NRSV)

While "the law" and other means of controlling behavior could only curb the effects of sin, the Incarnate One actually cures. His cure involved choosing us fully.

This is why Jesus had to get up close and personal with sin, to share the disease of alienation. This is why Jesus suffered betrayal and abandonment from his friends. His own body was affected. This is why in Scripture you see Jesus getting hungry and tired. He weeps, he bleeds, he even dies.

> *Slide*: He was despised and rejected by others;
>   a man of suffering and acquainted with infirmity;
>   and as one from whom others hide their faces
>   he was despised, and we held him of no account.
>   Surely he has borne our infirmities and carried our
>   diseases;
>   yet we accounted him stricken, struck down by God, and
>   afflicted.
>   But he was wounded for our transgressions,
>   crushed for our iniquities;
>   upon him was the punishment that made us whole,
>   and by his bruises we are healed.
>   All we like sheep have gone astray;
>   we have all turned to our own way,
>   and the LORD has laid on him the iniquity of us all.
>   (Isa. 53:3–6 NRSV)

THE TREATMENT PLAN

The incarnation was thus the necessary first stage in God's treatment plan for sin.

> *Message slide (built up in stages, as matched below)*:
>   God's Treatment Plan
>   Stage 1: Incarnation (ingesting the virus)
>   Stage 2: Crucifixion (achieving the cure)
>   Stage 3: Resurrection (releasing the cure)
>   Stage 4: Final Reunion (fully realizing the healing)

Stage 1. The incarnation leads naturally to the crucifixion. Having already ingested our sinful condition, Jesus on the cross withstands the virus's attack at its extreme. On the cross, he personally holds together what sin would rip apart: God and humanity. As God, he strains against every temptation to reject humanity: here he is God being crucified by mere humans—what more legitimate time for God to reject humanity! But from the God side, he succeeds, to the end loving humanity, even his human enemies. As human, he strains against every temptation to reject his Father God: what more legitimate time for a human to claim that God has abandoned him! But from the human side, he succeeds, committing himself to the Father even with his last breath.

Stage 2. And thus he achieves the cure. He resists sin and keeps God and humanity together against the greatest strain. He hangs on to both and thus unites both. That's why we proclaim that at the cross Jesus decisively achieved the cure for sin. Alienation finally met its ultimate resistance there in the person of Jesus. The antibody to sin was produced there.

We receive the cure as we spiritually take Jesus into us, receiving his donated body and blood. This is why every week here at the River Church we physically celebrate that spiritual donation in communion: we regularly enact sharing in the cure Jesus achieved at the cross.

Stage 3. The crucifixion then leads to the next part of the plan, the resurrection of Jesus. In the resurrection of Jesus, God releases the cure to the world. Because of the resurrection, there is a new form of life bursting out in this world: a life that has endured every form of alienation, has overcome it in its extreme, and is now spreading from person to person. This is why the resurrection historically is so closely associated with the good news of Jesus spreading throughout the world.

Stage 4. Finally, the gospel promises us a final reunion with Jesus when he returns to earth. The final reunion, by the way, takes place on earth when Jesus returns here. It is not, as so often mistakenly portrayed, when we go away from earth to heaven. This final stage is when all of us who follow Jesus as our Savior and Lord are completely united with Jesus. This is when all alienation is finally and completely eradicated. All alienation—all disunion—is eradicated because the final and ultimate reunion takes place.

WHERE WE ARE IN THE PLAN

This promise of fully realized healing comes at this last stage, in our final reunion with Jesus. In the first three stages, the gospel tells us, God in Christ decisively achieved victory over the disease; sin actually met its match in the incarnation, crucifixion, and resurrection. And yet there is this curious gap, this time of waiting, until the final stage where we are promised full and final pain relief. We currently live in the interval between stage 3 and stage 4. In this time, the symptoms of sin still occur. I still have hepatitis. There is this strange interval between the decisive achievement of the cure, its release into the world, and the ultimate disappearance of all the symptoms.

We need to be absolutely clear that this delay exists if we are to enroll in God's treatment plan. Unfortunately, there are a lot of preachers out there who are essentially selling a narcotic: Jesus as a magic pill that will make all the pain disappear immediately, right when you sign up. Don't get me wrong: there are a lot of benefits, a lot of even pain relief that occurs when you do sign up. But the full realization, the complete removal of all the symptoms is not promised until the end. And if we don't get that clear in our mind and heart, we will have misplaced our hope.

But understandably, you might still ask, "Why is that? Why does God set up this interval?"

Different Christian thinkers have given a variety of explanations for the delay. Many in the early church assumed that the wait would be brief, and hence, there's not a lot of theological reflection on this in the New Testament. The great theologian Augustine of Hippo stated that this gap was meant to give more people the opportunity to choose to follow Jesus before he returned. Others have simply said that it is one of the mysteries of God's plan and a matter of faith.

If I were to venture my own answer, it seems to me that this interval serves as God's invitation to humanity to enroll in his treatment plan as more than just a patient, but also as a fellow health worker. We certainly are first and foremost patients who receive this cure that Jesus alone achieved at the cross. And the release of this cure really is the work of the resurrected Jesus; it does not ultimately depend on any of our contributions. Nevertheless, the gospel invites us to participate in what Jesus has already achieved and is achieving. We didn't make the antibody, but we do have a role in administering it to the world. And while Jesus is the one ultimately releasing to the world his own self, his resurrected life, we do announce his presence.

Sharing in Jesus's healing of the world in this way naturally grows out of the healing achieved in Jesus's death and resurrection. If the disease is alienation from God and his purposes, it only makes sense that healing involves being reunited to his purposes for the world. Sharing in his purposes for the world is inseparable from sharing in the Incarnate One, who died and rose again. This is why the apostle Paul described his work in administering and announcing God's cure in the following language:

> *Slide*: I want to know Christ and the power of his resurrection and the sharing of his sufferings by becoming like him in his death, and so, somehow, to attain to the resurrection from the dead. (Phil. 3:10 NRSV; 3:11 NIV)

May this be the prayer of our community this Christmas season.

Recovering the Scandal of the Cross lists theological and missiological guidelines for atonement theology that we gleaned from the New Testament authors as they wrote about the atonement in the context of mission in the first century.[2] I reviewed these guidelines in the first chapter of this book, and I hope you have observed them in use by the various contributors to this volume.

What we saw in the New Testament, we also see in this sermon. Curtis Chang clearly communicates our acute need as humans. In his terminology, we suffer from alienation—deeply and broadly. He does not, however, simply present salvation from, but also salvation for; his proclamation includes a call for us to be reunited with God's purposes and join in God's mission. He clearly presents salvation as God's action in and through Christ. Just as the problem of alienation is universal, so also the saving work of the cross and resurrection is proclaimed to all—not just to people of one ethnic group, in a certain area of San Jose, or with a particular type of job.

Chang contextualizes well. He is aware of his audience. The viral metaphor of the cross is an attempt to draw on language that his increasingly diverse community could recognize from its use in their world. The congregation includes people who are HIV positive or hepatitis carriers, as well as biotech and health-care professionals.

The cross is central in this sermon—a centrality that Chang highlights by linking it to their weekly communion celebration. The importance of the incarnation, however, is powerfully present as well. His description of his wife's still choosing him in spite of his hepatitis and other health concerns, and his using a virus as a metaphor for the human condition of alienation—all these set up his discussion of the incarnation in a way that helps the listener sense both the huge cost to Jesus as well as Jesus's tremendous commitment. Jesus willingly exposed himself fully to our infection so that he could "donate his body and blood to everyone else," dying in our place. This is a metaphor of substitutionary atonement that integrally links Jesus's life to the cross and atonement in a much fuller and more profound way than simply stating that Jesus lived a sinless life and hence could pay the penalty humans owed to God. Chang's metaphor also includes the resurrection in a way that penal satisfaction does not, or at least does not require.

In this sermon Chang models for us the possibility of developing new and contextually relevant atonement metaphors that are biblically and theologically richer and deeper than many stories and images of atonement that evangelists and churches commonly use today.

19

Absorbing the Three D's of Death

Steve Todd

The need to use contemporary images of the atonement is especially important in evangelism and with new converts unfamiliar with biblical terms and images. Steve Todd addresses people from those categories in the discipleship/membership class at Horizons Community Church. It is a United Methodist Church in Lincoln, Nebraska, that describes its mission as leading seekers and doubters to experience transformation as devoted followers of Christ. In this chapter Todd describes how he explains sin in concrete terms from everyday life and how he uses a scene from a recent film to develop an image of atonement.

Todd's presentation parallels Chang's sermon in the previous chapter. It is, however, distinct in significant ways that I explore at the chapter's end.

In our discipleship/membership course we regularly split the participants into groups of four to six people to look at Scripture passages together. During one session we invite them to look at various Scriptures on why Jesus came and ask them to reflect on questions such as these: "What was the problem? What is the human condition? What are the consequences? What's the remedy? How does Jesus make a difference? How do we respond?"

When the groups are finished, I lead a large-group review of what they have found in their assigned passages. The section below is part of what I say in that review.

The result of our sin is death—and it is not just physical death, although mortality is one of the consequences of sin entering the human picture. The death we bring on ourselves operates at multiple levels, which I think of as the three D's.

Distance is the death of our relationship with God and our relationships with each other. From my own experience I know that I can so easily mess up my relationships and create distance.

Distortion is the death of a healthy understanding of ourselves, so that we no longer see ourselves as valued children of God, imprinted with our heavenly Father's spiritual DNA. We become twisted, distorted versions of the persons we were meant to be.

Destruction is death at the societal level, injustices that destroy people and our planet.

Jesus took all of that distance, distortion, and destruction that we have brought on ourselves, and on the cross he absorbed it into himself, carrying that burden across the threshold of physical death. It is a burden that we cannot carry across that threshold; it would crush us. But God, through Jesus, carried it for us.

When I imagine Jesus carrying my self-imposed distance, distortion, and destruction, there is an image I recall from the movie *The Green Mile*, based on the Stephen King novel. A wrongly accused and condemned inmate, John Coffey (played by Michael Clarke Duncan), possesses healing powers. In one particular scene, he opens his mouth inches away from a woman dying from the final stages of cancer. She opens her mouth, and a swarm of demonic-like flies flow out of her and into him. In some spiritual way, he ingests them. He is weakened for a bit, but then he opens his mouth again and expels the flies into the air along with their evil, poison, and sickness. She has been made whole, and he is whole, as well. John Coffey possesses the power and the purity to do this: his initials are J. C.

That image helps me understand what Jesus accomplished for us on the cross. He absorbed our death—the distance, distortion, and destruction—into himself. The personal cost to him was so great that he died. But death does not win, and in his resurrection he expels that poison, rendering it harmless. As we reach out to him and receive him by faith, we are made whole. Only the Healer has the power and purity to do this.

The session concludes with an evangelistic appeal in which class members silently indicate during a prayer whether they have previously received Christ, have not yet received Christ before today but would like to do so, or are coming closer but are not quite ready to receive Christ at this time. I lead in a prayer for those who make each response.

———

Theologically, Steve Todd's presentation repeats atonement themes we have already seen in this book. Using Steve Taylor's diamond analogy, we would say that Todd leads us to look at a face of the diamond we have already examined. He communicates the saving significance of the cross and resurrection through presenting Jesus Christ as fully absorbing the evil of sin and through that action providing healing. There is also a sense of Jesus as representative human, who heals not just one person, but has the potential of healing all.

The theological themes are not new, but I include this presentation in the book because other aspects are distinct. The setting and genre differ from other approaches in the book, as does the specific image he uses from the movie. I also appreciate the brevity of this presentation. The combination of his easily understood and remembered description of sin and death and the metaphor of healing and freedom through the cross sets up, in a clear and engaging way, his evangelistic invitation.

20

Go and Do Likewise

Mark D. Baker

I have already offered numerous comments and observations at the end of each chapter, and perhaps all that I need to say at this point is this: "Go and do likewise" (Luke 10:37). My hope and prayer is that the presentations in this book have helped you imagine the possibility of developing new metaphors of atonement, and inspired you to do so. I trust that what the contributors to this book have modeled will offer guidance as you seek to develop images of the atonement that are biblical and contextual—ones that provide alternatives to the penal satisfaction images, which are so common.

In addition to trying new images and stories of the saving significance of the cross and resurrection, readers can borrow and adapt ideas from the presentations in this book. As I have stated at various points, not all metaphors will work in the same way in all contexts. Your context, however, may match up well with some of the presentations in this book, and some others can be adapted to your context. I have borrowed images from this book and fitted them to contexts ranging from Asheville, North Carolina, to Asunción, Paraguay; from audiences of seminary students in Fresno, California, to *campesinos* (peasant farmers) in Honduras. I encourage you to do the same.

One image I have borrowed and now will borrow again is Steve Taylor's diamond image from chapter 10. The saving significance of the cross and resurrection, the message of atonement, is like a many-faceted diamond. I want to reiterate my conviction that rather than developing an explanation seeking to convey the combined meaning of all the faces of the diamond, we are much better off, especially in proclamation, to use a diversity of images and metaphors focusing on different facets of the diamond. No contribution in this book pretends to communicate the full salvific significance of the cross, nor does the book itself claim to have covered all the facets. In their own ways the contributors, however, have each sought to help us more profoundly experience the reality of a facet that we might obscure or even lose if we treated one image or explanation as being *the* message of the atonement.

To take the diamond metaphor one step further, we could say that, in addition to the atonement facets, there are other facets to the scandal of the cross. As I stated in the first chapter, this book intentionally focuses on the theme of salvation. There are, however, other significant facets to include as we proclaim the scandal of the cross. For instance the authors of a recent book, *StormFront: The Good News of God*, ask: Why did the early Christian preachers throw the offense of the cross into the face of the world? Why didn't they downplay the scandalous and shameful way Jesus died—like a common criminal, a rebellious slave, a subversive—and simply state that he died for our sins? The authors offer a few suggestions on why the early preachers explicitly kept the cross of Jesus as central in the proclamation:

> The message of the cross means that the church is, in very fundamental ways, a community that radically calls into question the status quo. . . . The message of the cross jars Christians loose from normal assumptions and expectations. . . . It suggests that God's work in our lives emerges in the most surprising and unexpected ways: in the brokenness, the darkness, the loneliness of our lives. . . . The cross shatters our conventional understandings of what it means to love. . . . It calls us to a profoundly different kind of life: loving, trusting, and risking more deeply than we otherwise would have thought possible.[1]

We could continue adding other facets to the significance of the scandal of the cross, such as unpacking the last line of the above quote and detailing what the cross models for us and how it challenges us, such as servanthood and nonretaliation. Or, heading in a different direction, by reflecting on Luther's call to develop a theology of the cross. This would not be an atonement theology about the cross, but a theology that intentionally uses the cross as a central lens influencing every aspect of our theology.

By focusing on the atonement and the salvation facets of the scandal of the cross, I in no way mean to downplay the importance of these other facets. In fact, my hope is that if we can move away from having penal satisfaction as *the one* full explanation of the saving significance of the cross and include other metaphors and images like those in this book, we will create more space for hearing the other facets of the scandal of the cross. I hope that we not only hear them but also understand them as integrally related to the salvation facets of the cross.

May the Spirit guide us and use us as we seek to communicate the full and deep meaning of the cross and resurrection of Jesus in our various contexts today.

For further resources on the atonement visit www.mbseminary .edu/baker and click on "resources on the atonement."

Notes

Chapter 1: Contextualizing the Scandal of the Cross

1. See the phrases "powerful in words and deeds" and "to redeem Israel" (Luke 24:19, 21 NIV), also used in Acts 7:22 in Stephen's description of Moses, as well as the phrase, "before God and all the people," an echo from Moses's epitaph in Deut. 34:10–12.

2. The usual translation of *mōria* as "folly" (1 Cor. 1:18 RSV) or "foolishness" (NIV, NRSV) is probably too weak. See Martin Hengel, *Crucifixion in the Ancient World and the Folly of the Message of the Cross* (Philadelphia: Fortress, 1977), 1; Justin writes: "They say that our madness (*mania*) consists in the fact that we put a crucified man in second place after the unchangeable and eternal God, the Creator of the world" (*1 Apol.* 13.4).

3. Joel B. Green and Mark D. Baker, *Recovering the Scandal of the Cross: Atonement in New Testament and Contemporary Contexts* (Downers Grove, IL: InterVarsity, 2000; Carlisle: Paternoster, 2003).

4. C. M. Tuckett, "Atonement in the NT," in *Anchor Bible Dictionary*, ed. D. N. Freedman (New York: Doubleday, 1992), 1:518–22, esp. 518.

5. Anselm of Canterbury was the first to fully develop a satisfaction theory of the atonement in the eleventh century, in his book *Why God Became Man: Cur Deus homo*, trans. Jasper Hopkins and Herbert Richardson (Queenston, ON: E. Mellen, 1985). That is not to say, however, that themes related to that theory were absent from the writings of theologians before Anselm. Hans Boersma lists examples and urges us to make neither too much nor too little out of the presence of these themes before Anselm: see his *Violence, Hospitality, and the Cross: Reappropriating the Atonement Tradition* (Grand Rapids: Baker, 2004), 158–63.

6. Chapter 5 of *Recovering the Scandal* covers this material in more depth and takes the approach of focusing on representative thinkers in the different categories.

7. Gustaf Aulén, *Christus Victor: An Historical Study of the Three Main Types of the Idea of the Atonement* (London: SPCK, 1953).

8. Gregory of Nyssa described Jesus as bait that hid the hook; alternative approaches from that general era include Irenaeus, Origen, and Gregory of Nazianzus. Two contemporary examples of a reworking of *Christus Victor* are Darby Kathleen Ray, *Deceiving the Devil: Atonement, Abuse, and Ransom* (Cleveland: Pilgrim, 1998); and J. Denny Weaver, *The Nonviolent Atonement* (Grand Rapids: Eerdmans, 2001).

9. E.g., victory over the powers of evil: Gal. 4:3–9; Eph. 2:14–16; 3:7–13; Col. 2:13–15; ransom/redemption: Matt. 20:28; 1 Cor. 6:20; 7:23; Gal. 4:3–9; 1 Tim. 2:6; Titus 2:14; Rev. 5:9.

10. For a fuller description and assessment of Anselm's work, including ways he is different from and avoids some of the problems of penal satisfaction that he gets blamed for, see Green and Baker, *Recovering the Scandal*, 126–36. For Anselm's book, see note 5.

11. Peter Abelard (Pierre Abélard), *Expositio in Epistolam ad Romanos* (*Exposition of the Epistle to the Romans*), in Latin and German, trans. Rolf Peppermüller (New York: Herder, 2000).

12. E.g., Rom. 5:8; 8:32–39; 1 John 3:16; 4:10.

13. At times, Abelard does seem to recognize that even after being awakened to love by Jesus's example, humans will fall short and need the merit of Christ's perfect love. For example, he wrote: "That [Jesus] . . . might supply from his own what was wanting in our merits. . . . Otherwise what great thing did his holiness merit, if it availed only for his own, and not for others' salvation" (cited in H. D. McDonald, *The Atonement of the Death of Christ: In Faith, Revelation, and History* [Grand Rapids: Baker, 1985], 177).

14. Green and Baker, *Recovering the Scandal*, 169.

15. C. Norman Kraus, "From Biblical Intentions to Theological Conceptions, Reply to T. Finger," *Conrad Grebel Review* 8 (1990): 213.

16. There are presentations in this book that have affinity with the moral influence theory, but they are images, proclamations of an aspect of the saving significance of the cross, and do not rule out presenting a substitutionary image as well. This contrasts with a moral influence theory presented as *the* explanation of the cross.

17. Just as the readers of this book are at different points on this spectrum, not all contributors in this book are necessarily at the same point on this spectrum as I am—the second. Some may be at this position (the fourth) or the previous one.

18. Hans Boersma, "The Disappearance of Punishment: Metaphors, Models, and the Meaning of the Atonement," *Books & Culture* 9, no. 2 (March/April 2003): 32. He quotes from Green and Baker, *Recovering the Scandal*, 86.

19. Boersma, *Violence, Hospitality, and the Cross*; Kevin J. Vanhoozer, "The Atonement in Postmodernity," in *The Glory of the Atonement*, ed. Charles E. Hill and Frank A. James III (Downers Grove, IL: InterVarsity, 2004), 367–404.

20. Boersma, *Violence, Hospitality, and the Cross*, 163. He does not deny that the cross has a juridical character; rather, he critiques how it has been overly emphasized: "When I speak about the juridicizing of the atonement, I have in mind a form of reductionism that limits the divine-human relationship to judicial

categories, and that views the cross solely in terms of laws, infractions, judicial pronouncements, forgiveness, and punishments" (p. 164).

21. Kevin J. Vanhoozer argues that God's wrath need not be emotion-laden and that it is unfair for us to caricature penal substitution as teaching thus ("Atonement in Postmodernity," 376). I agree with Vanhoozer that we need not understand God's wrath as ever on the verge of striking out, and acknowledge that some well-argued explanations of penal substitution avoid this problem. That does not, however, change the reality that this view of God's wrath pervades Christian communities, at least in North America, and how closely people at the popular level link this view of God's wrath with penal substitution theory. As Hans Boersma states, "Even if we conclude that the charges against traditional atonement theology are based on caricatures or misunderstandings, this still does not absolve us from the responsibility to deal with the issues" (*Violence, Hospitality, and the Cross*, 42). I am working to "deal with the issues" through presenting alternatives to penal satisfaction; my hope is that others would not simply dismiss my work at a scholarly level by saying I am critiquing a caricature or straw man, but will work in their own ways to attack this "straw man," which is robustly alive at the popular level.

22. Frederica Mathewes-Green, "The Meaning of Christ's Suffering," *Books & Culture* 10, no. 2 (March/April 2004): 29. For a contemporary example of atonement proclamation from this perspective, see her contribution in chapter 3 of this book.

23. Ibid., 28. We make similar points with regard to "ransom" in Green and Baker, *Recovering the Scandal*, as we develop the argument by using biblical texts: see 38–43, 93–94, 100–102.

24. Raymund Schwager, *Must There Be Scapegoats? Violence and Redemption in the Bible* (New York: Crossroad, 2000), 206–7.

25. William Placher, "Christ Takes Our Place: Rethinking Atonement," *Interpretation* 53, no. 1 (1999): 16.

26. For an excellent, brief summary of arguments for the various translations and the theological ramifications of those readings, see Judith M. Gundry-Volf, "Expiation, Propitiation, Mercy Seat," in *Dictionary of Paul and His Letters*, ed. Gerald F. Hawthorne, Ralph P. Martin, and Daniel G. Reid (Downers Grove, IL: InterVarsity, 1993), 279–84.

27. For a short description of these differing concepts of justice, see Richard B. Hays, "Justification," in *Anchor Bible Dictionary*, 3:1129–33. For a longer discussion, see James D. G. Dunn and Alan M. Suggate, *The Justice of God: A Fresh Look at the Old Doctrine of Justification by Faith* (Grand Rapids: Eerdmans, 1993).

28. Green and Baker, *Recovering the Scandal*, 221.

Chapter 2: Deeper Magic Conquers Death and the Powers of Evil

1. C. S. Lewis, *The Lion, the Witch and the Wardrobe* (New York: Harper Trophy, 1994), 169–71.

2. Ibid., 177–78.

3. Ibid., 178–79.

4. C. S. Lewis, *Mere Christianity* (New York: Macmillan, 1958), 46.

Chapter 3: Rising Victorious

1. Frederica Mathewes-Green, "Rising Victorious," *Christianity and the Arts* 5, no. 1 (1998): 6–10.
2. For an overview and assessment of this approach, see Green and Baker, *Recovering the Scandal*, 117–25.

Chapter 5: A Different Story

1. *I See Satan Fall like Lightning* is one of a number of books by René Girard that explores the relation between his thought and the atonement (Maryknoll, NY: Orbis, 2001).
2. For an introduction to Girard, see Gil Baillie, *Violence Unveiled* (New York: Crossroad, 1995). Among those who have built upon, and gone beyond, his work in relation to the atonement are James Allison, *Raising Abel* (New York: Crossroad, 2000); Anthony W. Bartlett, *Cross Purposes: The Violent Grammar of Christian Atonement* (Harrisburg, PA: Trinity Press International, 2001); Raymund Schwager, *Must There Be Scapegoats? Violence and Redemption in the Bible* (New York: Crossroad, 2000).

Chapter 7: The Forgiveness of Sins

1. This work was originally published in a book of sermons by Rowan Williams, *Open to Judgment* (London: Darton, Longman & Todd, 1994); *A Ray of Darkness* (Cambridge, MA: Cowley Publications, 1995).
2. I do not mean to imply that this is his theological approach. I see his theological thinking clearly rooted in God's revelation in Jesus and centered at the cross, that starting point, and the scandalous nature of a theology with that foundation is in fact clearly evident in other sermons in this same collection.

Chapter 8: Atonement

1. Raymund Schwager, *Jesus in the Drama of Salvation: Toward a Biblical Doctrine of Redemption* (New York: Crossroad, 1999).
2. A number of people read drafts of this parable and made helpful suggestions. Some may recognize a line or a word that they recommended; others made a significant number of suggestions, including Julia Baker, Rick Bartlett, Kristin Fast, Lisa Washio, Dan Whitmarsh, and Bill Yaccino.
3. Schwager offers an insightful interpretation of Jesus's parables of judgment that contributed to my understanding of the rejection/judgment dynamic I describe in these two sentences: *Jesus in the Drama of Salvation*, 53–69, 195–96.

Chapter 9: Made New by One Man's Obedience

1. Paul J. Achtemeier, *Romans*, Interpretation (Louisville: John Knox, 1985), 102.
2. By this statement I do not mean to imply that Paul, in other places, articulates what today is called a penal substitutionary theory of the atonement. As I have written elsewhere, in Romans 3 Paul portrays God as demonstrating righteousness not through a retributive punishment that allows him to "justly" forgive sins, but

by providing salvation through Christ Jesus and thus being just/righteous in the sense of being faithful to his covenant promises. See Richard B. Hays, "Psalm 143 and the Logic of Romans 3," *Journal of Biblical Literature* 99 (1980): 107–15; idem, *Echoes of Scripture in the Letters of Paul* (New Haven: Yale University Press, 1989), 52–53; idem, "Justification," *Anchor Bible Dictionary*, 3:1129–33.

Chapter 10: Participation and an Atomized World

1. The introductory image of the diamond occurred to me as I read the book by Morna D. Hooker, *Not Ashamed of the Gospel: New Testament Interpretations of the Death of Christ* (Carlisle: Paternoster, 1994).

2. The list of the diamond's faces is based on chapter titles from John Driver, *Understanding the Atonement for the Mission of the Church* (Scottdale, PA: Herald Press, 1986).

3. Sir Edmund Hillary (1919–) is New Zealand's most accomplished explorer, gaining world renown in 1953 as the first person (with his Sherpa guide Tenzing Norgay) to climb Mt. Everest. In 1958 Sir Edmund became the first person to drive overland to the South Pole.

4. The movie is available on video and DVD from Columbia Tristar Home Entertainment. I have drawn on both the video and the original book, Witi Ihimaera, *The Whale Rider* (Auckland: Reed, 1987).

5. Dietrich Bonhoeffer, "Outline for a Book," in *Letters and Papers from Prison* (New York: Touchstone, 1997), 382.

6. Christopher Marshall, *Beyond Retribution: A New Testament Vision for Justice, Crime, and Punishment* (Grand Rapids: Eerdmans, 2001), 61 (italics in the original).

7. For example, see Irenaeus, *Against Heresies* 3.18.7 and 3.19.1. For a brief overview of Irenaeus's recapitulation theory, see *Recovering the Scandal*, 119–21. For a more in-depth explanation of it, see Boersma, *Violence, Hospitality, and the Cross*. Boersma employs Irenaeus's thought in creative and helpful ways throughout his book.

Chapter 11: The Cross as Prophetic Action

1. For example, several prophets tell the future in hopes that their prognostications *won't* come true: their nondeterministic forecasts of judgment are intended as ultimatums to persuade God's people to repent, thus avoiding the foretold judgment. In other words, if the prophecy fulfills its intended function, it doesn't need to come true (see Jonah, for example).

2. After completing the chapter, the reader may wish to come back and ponder this question: To what degree does the dominant evangelical understanding of atonement today reflect the dominance of our theology and religious life by the priestly mind-set, and a loss of the prophetic?

3. Thanks to Leonard Sweet for the contrast between seeing God as audience versus humanity as audience, and to Dallas Willard and N. T. Wright for stimulating a number of insights reflected in this sermon.

4. Brian D. McLaren, *The Story We Find Ourselves In* (San Francisco: Jossey-Bass, 2003), 106–7; see also 153 and 170.

Chapter 13: The Family Table

1. For a more in-depth discussion of shame and the atonement, see chap. 6, "Removing Alienating Shame," in Green and Baker, *Recovering the Scandal*.

Chapter 14: Jesus, the Ultimate Outsider

1. Ray S. Anderson, *The Gospel according to Judas* (Colorado Springs: Helmers & Howard, 1991), 21.

Chapter 16: Present

1. Originally published in *Radix* 31, no. 1; "Present" was subsequently collected in Luci Shaw, *What the Light Was Like* (La Porte, IN: WordFarm, 2006).

Chapter 17: Salvation through the Sacrifice of God's Firstborn Son

1. For a survey of the role of blood and sacrifices in African cultures and contextual reflection on their relation to discipleship and theology, including the atonement, see David W. Shenk, *Justice, Reconciliation, and Peace in Africa*, rev. ed. (Nairobi: Uzima, 1997). For another example of sacrificial imagery used to proclaim the saving significance of the cross in a different African culture see Green and Baker, *Recovering the Scandal*, 187–91.

2. See the description of a Japanese pastor's frustration with not being able to understand the penal satisfaction explanation of the atonement because the legal and judicial categories were foreign to him, in Green and Baker, *Recovering the Scandal*, chap. 6.

Chapter 18: He Shared Our Aches

1. Green and Baker, *Recovering the Scandal*, 191–94.
2. Ibid., 112–15.

Chapter 20: Go and Do Likewise

1. James V. Brownson et al., *StormFront: The Good News of God* (Grand Rapids: Eerdmans, 2003), 62–63.

Scripture Index

Subject Index